Eva's Journey

Escape From Tyranny to the Switzerland of South America

Isabel Balboa

To Debbie and Brenda, the radiance in Eva's eyes, that they may pass on Eva's rich legacy to her grandchildren, aunts, uncles, cousins and others generations to come...

Eva's Journey: Escape From Tyranny to the Switzerland of South America
By Isabel Balboa

ImPress Publishing Services
Orlando, Florida
NewhouseCreativeGroup.com
2026, Isabel Balboa

Names: Balboa, Isabel
Title: Eva's Journey: Escape From Tyranny to the Switzerland of South America / by Isabel Balboa
Description: Orlando, FL | ImPress Publishing Services. | Summary: The story of the turbulent life of a tenacious Holocaust survivor who overcame disappointments, fears and losses to prosper in a new continent.
ISBN 978-1-945493-73-7 (paperback)

Contents

Eva's Journey

Prologue

"For I know the plans I have for you, declares the Lord, plans to prosper you and not harm you, plans to give you hope and a future."

-Jeremiah 29:11

In the late seventies, I met a sophisticated and vivacious woman Eva through my co-worker Deborah at the bank where we worked. Debbie, as she liked to be called, introduced me to her mother, a businesswoman and private banker. Debbie's mom had just flown in for a quick visit from her homeland, Uruguay, and I became curious of her career path as a businesswoman living in South America. As we spoke, I observed her accent to be distinctly

European. Like Debbie she had fiery red hair. In our conversations she shared that she had been born in Vienna but lived most of her life in the Republic of Uruguay. Her family had been forced to escape Europe and settle in Uruguay after the antisemitic Nazi takeover of Austria during World War II.

Eva Roth—in her fifties when I met her—had moxie and a seemingly innate shrewdness for business and finance. She spoke flawless Spanish, as well as English with a slight European accent. She could also understand and converse in German and Yiddish. Her manner of dress reflected mindfulness, sophistication, and affluence. Her hair carefully coiffed, complexion subtly made-up and her hands naturally manicured. I sensed the pieces which dressed her neck, wrists, and hands were smartly curated—not insubstantial.

She spoke confidently, displaying a breadth of knowledge and understanding about a broad range of topics that drew you into her gaze. Her demeanor beckoned attention. She spoke in polished English with precision and Spanish with the rhythmic but refined Southern Cone accent. Her skin appeared bronzed by years of sunbathing and travels to exotic beaches and resorts around the world. She smoked while we walked and talked, balancing her cigarette with her lips so that the ash remained intact until she delicately reached for the ashtray at just the precise moment.

Eva typified a truly cosmopolitan woman. She had been born in Austria to a successful and established Jewish family and considered herself a member of the Uruguayan Jewish "*colectividad*" (community). She had travelled extensively for business and pleasure and knew of countries and cultures unfamiliar to most people. I had never met anyone with such complexity of character and background.

This woman with whom I crossed paths shared the details of her arduous youth in the advent of World War II leading to her family's remarkable escape to South America. During our conversations, I learned of her burdens and apprehensions, but also her strength of character and indomitable will. Throughout the course of Eva's life, she chronicled her life through notebooks, photographs, and journals detailing her life's tipping points. Interviews and conversations over two decades along with her firsthand sources form her biography. Eva's journey is the story of unpredictable tipping points that engulfed the lives of most European Jews who survived World War II.

During our friendship, Eva shared how she and her family, at great risk escaped Europe. Tenaciously they adapted and flourished in a new culture and made Uruguay their new homeland. Eva's preserved accounts of her family's life together with interviews and conversations over two decades provided the framework for this book. In those she shared the adjustments to life in a different culture, as well as her joys in being part of a vibrant Jewish community. Her life was bereft by losses and disappointments but also gratified by tremendous personal victories and the joy of kinship and indominable family ties.

ANTWERP

THE GATHERING STORM

Come with me, open your senses, and capture perhaps a glimpse of what they witnessed and what they endured.

The sun emerged over the horizon as a dimly lit, opaque fireball of evanescent hues of orange and yellow. Dense fog enveloped the port city—the ships and cargo imperceptible. All around, a cacophony of foghorns ushered the perilous opening into the port. The sounds of stevedores, fishmongers, pushcart vendors, and cargo being hoisted all merged as one revealing the port's morning dance. In this bustling port of Antwerp Eva, a young child and her family would find a way out of Europe.

They found themselves in the port of Antwerp. A place unusual in its topography. The narrow mouth of the port stretched for more than a mile. Its crevices unveiled an intersection of swamps, underbrush, moorings, and docks. In the 1930s, yet another war approached the European continent, and the port of Antwerp would make its mark on history. At the time, Antwerp ranked second only to Rotterdam in size and movement of cargo in continental Europe. This inland port connects to the Scheldt River, allowing for the movement of cargo inland. In the days preceding the war, marshes surrounding its entrance also provided great cover for smugglers, travelers, and traders in human cargo.

Slipping between the haggard port workers and the watchful eyes of those in various uniforms and insignias, a mass of humanity circulated. Strapping young men with heavy loads on their shoulders moved briskly along the pathways leading to the moorings. They whisked by old men with withered skin and furrowed brows arching their backs and looking downward to remain unseen. The mélange of classes, diverse cultures, vendors, and peoples of questionable backgrounds filled the landscape leading to the docks. The morning chill and misty veil pierced the tattered coats of those moving about making discreet inquiries around the port concerning destinations, fares, and berth availability. Most ships in the port these days were commercial vessels loading and unloading under the boot of an ever-growing military presence. Eva's father, Walter, stood out as a handsome young businessman from another country and culture.

In the early spring of 1939, the drums of war resonated throughout the capitals of Europe. For those searching for a way out, there were no clear pathways. No one knew if the next ship, or any ship, would take on another load of steerage. Many euphemisms described travelers those days, but there were clearly identifiable groups: the hunters, and the hunted, the exploited, and the desperate.

Every day, as the German boots and instruments of destruction moved southwest at a menacing pace, thousands gathered around the port city of Antwerp. Eva and her family now formed part of the population in Belgium's port spilling over to surrounding towns, swelling to over a million in a matter of weeks. Most of those, predominantly Jews, Slavic people, and people of color, coming into the port had a singular objective: find a way out of Europe. Each day, more families arrived, some coming from Rotterdam or Cherbourg where passage eluded most passenger liners. Eva's uncle and aunt, Benno and Gertrude Bernkopf, found a way out on a passenger ship, *SS Veendam*, bound for New York. They reached New

York harbor on November 12, 1938, and made their lives in the United States. Eva and her young parents, Walter and Elsie Roth had a similar goal.

While the Roths considered how to flee Austria, most doors were closing throughout Europe. Antwerp offered a sliver of hope and the opportunity to begin anew wherever the Almighty would place them. In this harbor, there were cargo freighters, mixed liners, and commercial ships in abundance. Some did not appear seaworthy, but the haggard and weary desperate to get out could not afford to be selective knowing someone else would eagerly take their place.

Aware of the threats and the fears, of war, repression, and imprisonment to would-be passengers, a ship captain could easily profiteer from a few passengers; specifically, those with plentiful, valuable commodities and questionable visas. Most traveling those days had a connection, a "mensch," who had led them through this bastion. Walter and Elsie had help from their family and friends in Yugoslavia and Czechoslovakia. Through them, the Roths procured tourist visas from the Uruguayan consulate in Prague. In collaboration with other contacts, Walter now sought out a Flemish port worker who knew one of the Belgian officers of a freighter that made regular trips to South America, the *MS Copacabana*, operated by the

Compagnie Maritime Belge. Walter felt uncomfortable with the tenuous arrangements. He lacked precise information pertaining to the ship's arrival, departure date, pier, and slip. Even if he could find this elusive ship, he did not know how much space would be available. He feared the captain might choose not to take them or accept the negotiated price for the freight. In this place, neither Reichsmark nor Franc held much value. Gold and diamonds were the preferred currency of the day.

Walter would gladly negotiate passage on any ship heading away from Europe, but his family negotiated the fare prior to their departure. They obtained assurances that the *MS Copacabana*, a mixed-use liner, had a few cabins available. While in Austria, as he moved northwest, Walter heard of settlement possibilities in countries outside the European continent comprised of countries and cities that he could barely pronounce. He felt anxious and uncertain about leaving his family and the places familiar to him, yet his concern for his wife and young daughter surpassed his fears.

The war became imminent with the *Anschluss Oestreich* (annexation of Austria) in place. A mass exodus began within hours upon realization that Austria was now under German control. The race to leave Austria took on a fever pitch while German authorities sought to capitalize from those abandoning their homes and wealth. For Jews living throughout Europe, obtaining travel documents, a visa, an exit permit, and gaining passage out of the country required a contact on the inside, hard currency, assets, and a little luck. For the Roths, even with visas and currency reaching and embarking on "the" ship posed an even greater highwire act. They would need to find a way to escape Austria and get to the port one thousand kilometers (620 miles) from their home before all borders closed to them.

There were no guarantees that passage on the *Copacabana* would lead to departure. Frequently, authorities boarded and detained ships over questionable entries on the ship's manifest. Those prowling about with the power to board a ship and drag out passengers indiscriminately challenged documents merely for the appearance of questionable provenance. In the Roth's case, the documents procured in Austria and Prague contained flaws which could have foreclosed their travel.

The Roths could not have known upon entering Antwerp that the spot of their departure would be key to the ultimate liberation of Europe five years later. In this port, the Allied armies fought the battle of the Scheldt, liberating Belgian towns adjacent to the port of Antwerp. The Roths never imagined that, in those five years, western

Europe would be ravaged and starved, its cities' skylines nearly disappearing. In their naivete, the young family could not foresee the threats and challenges they would encounter.

Weeks prior to their departure, Walter's relatives in Czechoslovakia negotiated their passage on the *SS Copacabana*. This newer, Belgian-registered vessel made regular commercial trips between the ports of Antwerp and Bahia in Brazil with stops in Rio de Janeiro, Montevideo, and Buenos Aires. Walter hoped this would be the ship where he could find a sympathetic captain willing to make space for his wife and frail little girl. The *Copacabana*, if he could find it, offered a way out of what became a seemingly interminable and hellish nightmare for European Jews.

In the days leading to the declaration of war throughout Europe, the *Copacabana* traveled almost exclusively between Antwerp and Bahia in Brazil. Through conversations with others familiar with the port of Antwerp, Walter learned that, since the start of the war, this ship mainly delivered beef, and, after offloading its cargo, returned by way of Buenos Aires with light cargo and passengers. Walter hoped that with less cargo leaving than coming, space would be available for a few dozen passengers as valuable as any other cargo. The Roths and their family worried that despite paid passage and assurances, anyone could be subject to a bribe, and an intrepid crew member could always find someone willing to offer a higher or better offer. Getting on board with a young family would be difficult in the turbulent environment in which Walter found himself.

Walter deftly concealed the details of their proposed travel from Elsie to ease the fear which engulfed her. In this port city, overwhelmed with outsiders, animosity mounted concerning Jews, dubbed subversives, who were declared pariah spilling over from surrounding countries as they sought to outrun the invading German armies. While Walter walked the port making inquiries with the dock master, Eva and Elsie waited at their old, musty, and overcrowded guesthouse reeking with mold and the salty smells of the nearby port. Eva, a precocious child, would be difficult to control and keep quiet during a prolonged stay and an extended ocean crossing.

Walter knew to move quickly. They could not risk depleting their assets on food and lodging in this place where the black market thrived and prices rose daily. What they had in currency and jewelry, carefully guarded and hidden away in their persons and garments, would last only a short time. They anxiously sought to depart before any more doors would close to them. The whispers around the populace filling the guesthouses and shabby lodgings near the port all told of detentions and disappearances in the towns and cities they had left behind. None of these rumors could be verified. Walter thought it better to believe that they were false than to dwell on what might lie ahead if questioned or stopped. The Roths knew Benno and Gertrude had left through Rotterdam, but not what awaited them in New York.

Despite the uncertainties and the constant threat of arrest or deportation, Walter persevered. He felt there were few options available to him. The family could not return to Austria or even temporarily to Yugoslavia. Moreover, by the time they reached Antwerp, the German army had annexed Austria. Czechoslovakia had fallen to the Germans, as the Czech armies retreated without a fight. With blazing speed, the Germans occupied the territory beyond the Sudetenland all the way south to Brno in Czechoslovakia, a city close to the border with Austria. Most Jews remaining in Europe now lived in imminent danger either from the Germans, the fascist, or those sympathetic to their ideologies. Walter endeavored to find the *MS Copacabana* and, if necessary, any ship going away from the gathering storm.

Eva Roth, Vienna, Austria - 5 Years Old

Gumperdoffer Strasse Building - Circa 2024

Zwieback Residence at 144 Gumpendorfer Strasse

Transit station across the street from Zwieback Building

Site of Martin and Else Roth's apartment building at Turner Gasse 22. Appended to the Turner Synagogue established in 1871 and destroyed November 9-10, 1938.

A memorial was placed adjacent to the apartment building in November 2011 to mark the site of the synagogue.

WEIN

TAILORS CROSS PATHS

In the six years since their marriage, the world had changed radically. In the mid-1930s few Jews in Vienna (*Wein*), the urbane and elegant capital of Austria, foresaw the maelstrom that lie ahead. The rabbis and Zionist known to them tried to sound alarms among the Chabad houses, synagogues, and academic circles, but, regrettably, the fears of Jewish leaders over violence and antisemitic threats were met with incredulity by most.

Walter and Elsie met in Vienna in the late 1920s. Their parents lived only a few blocks apart, a fact they would learn as they courted. Walter's father, Martin Israel Roth, married Elsa Podzahradsky. After they wed, they moved to Turner Gasse, 22, Vienna where they brought up their son, Walter. They resided in an elegant apartment building, appended to the Turner Synagogue, the third largest synagogue in Vienna at the time. Martin lived and worked in a fashionable and well-maintained neighborhood filled with a mix of businesses and very private apartment dwellings. Their residence benefitted from an extra portion of grace as later events would show.

Viennese construction codes, dating back to the early 1800s, permitted no structure adjacent to a major street other than a Catholic church or house of worship. In the late 1800s, contractors embedded the elder Roths' apartment building into the synagogue to allow for its construction on the corner. Starting on November 9, 1938, a two-day rampage now known as *Kristallnacht* (night of broken glass) took place, nine months after the *Anschluss*, the annexation of Austria, by Germany. During the two-day rampage, as history chronicles with detail, Jews were killed, beaten, threatened, and ridiculed by unchecked mobs supporting the National Socialists in Austria. According to Yad Vashem, the World Holocaust Remembrance Center, 91 people were killed by the Nazis, and 30,000 men were arrested on Kristallnacht. 7,500 Jewish businesses, as well as cemeteries and educational centers were also vandalized and sustained significant damage. It is believed most synagogues and houses of worship in Vienna were burned or looted during those two nights, and the Turner Synagogue was among those sustaining significant damage. Perhaps by divine providence, G-d spared the adjacent apartment building to the synagogue from fire and destruction. No doubt, these events marked a turning point in antisemitic acts which should have persuaded Martin to consider departure from Austria for his family. Other Jews saw the threat and moved quickly to leave the country. In 1938 Austrian Jews numbered about 190,000, but by December of 1939 that population would dwindle to less than 60,000. Despite the Nuremburg laws in 1935 and mayhem of Kristallnacht, Martin delayed in seeking a haven. While Martin made no plans to depart Austria, he supported Walter in his desire to safeguard his family by charting a plan to escape.

Although Germany gave up much of its control in northern Europe after the Great War, the Treaty of Saint Germain brought forth the Republic of Austria. Though bruised and battered, Austria staved the communist threat from the east. A regionally splintered Austria returned to its world of aristocracy and commercial vibrancy. In the years that followed the cessation of the World War I, a resplendent Vienna sparkled at night, its cafes and music spilling over into the sidewalks. The landmark, *Reisenrad*, lit up the night while 30 immense gondolas ferried lovers, locals, and tourist from all backgrounds. The *Prater*, a large park with its landmark Ferris wheel and adjacent Praterstern railway station, swelled up with the arrival of every train. Trams competed with horse drawn carts and pushcarts as cinnamon, dung, and diesel fought for control of the air. This city gave the appearance of a most genteel place where intellectuals, artists and businessmen could all commune. Tall, smartly uniformed police walked their beat. The city provided comfort and luxuries in an economy propped up by foreign assistance and a League of Nations intent on keeping Germany in check.

Vienna cultivated a diverse population. Most European countries in the 19th and into the 20th century did not allow Jews to own land. Despite land ownership restrictions, Jews desiring to escape the dullness of country life gravitated towards cities and urban centers. They became professionals, academics, merchants, skilled workers, and entrepreneurs. For the Roths, the sale of quality, custom-made garments and textiles became a flourishing trade in the 20s. Walter found his niche as a purveyor in his family's shop, promoting and distributing their goods. He learned much of the trade from Martin, but he did not have his father's passion for the garment business. Although not the most ambitions, Walter became a good marketing agent, a skill that would serve him well after the war.

If Austria, and the course of history had not intervened, Walter would have served as an apprentice to his father and, in due time, inherit his father's business as the workmanship was well recognized and sought out by Jews and non-Jews, alike.

Although Jewish, Walter's parents lived in a mixed neighborhood for many years and considered themselves Austrians as much as Jews. By Austrian standards of the day, they lived comfortably.

Elsie's parents lived a more affluent and sophisticated lifestyle than the Roths. Oskar Zwieback, Elsie's father, married Gisela Deutsch in Vienna. Prior to the war, they lived at Gumpendorfer Strasse, 144 in Vienna; their home situated not far from significant Viennese landmarks, the *Reisenrad* and *Schoenbrunn* Palace. (The building at Gumperdorfer Strasse survived the war. Its exterior has been maintained and remains as it was in 1938. Presently the ground floor is filled by retail shops with the remaining floors serving as residences). Oskar succeeded in his commercial endeavors and, over the course of years, grew to be a collector of fine art and a lover of music. Born in Zagreb, Yugoslavia (now Croatia), his ancestral home was known as "Zweiback Palace". The home of Ignatz and Malvine Zwieback remains an impressive landmark in Osijek, Croatia. Like Martin however, Oskar and Gisela lived in Vienna most of their lives.

The Deutsch family owned a haberdashery, Bernard Deutsch & Co., Tailors. When Oskar married Gisela, he joined her family's tailor business. After their marriage, Oskar became a successful tailor in his own right and set up, Oskar Zweiback Moden House (high fashion clothiers). He may have also operated a side business called Martin's, perhaps jointly with Martin Roth. Zwieback's business operated in the same location as Bernard Deutsch and Company and sat on an ideal location on the corner of a busy business section of Vienna. The Zwiebacks resided in a large flat several floors above their tailor enterprise.

The Zwiebacks lived the life of Austrian bourgeois, the upper middle class. Gisela never worked outside her home. She dedicated herself to keeping an inviting home and setting her imprint on the more aristocratic Zwieback family. Their photos and mementos, which their daughter, Elsie kept throughout her life, reflect a life of pleasure and social standing. These photos showed the family vacationing during their summers and winters at various European resorts and venues through the years between the wars.

Oskar and Gisela Zwieback raised three children, Elsie being their youngest. Elsie's eldest sister and Annie who lived all of 16 years. Her middle sister, Gertrude, would marry Benno Bernkopf and outlive Elsie. Their father did well as a tailor of men's garments, and his avocation for art and artifacts most likely resulted in a sizable collection. They urgently needed to hide and discretely dispose of most of these before April 26, 1938, because a decree issued on that day required all Jewish citizens to report assets with a value of more than 5000 Reichsmark. The Zwiebacks foresight likely helped Walter and Elsie on their escape to Brno, Prague, Brussel, Antwerp and as they settled in Uruguay.

Since the Roths and Zwiebacks traveled in the same business circles, they likely sought to make a match for their children. This would have been customary at the time. No matter how the match came about, it proved successful. These two fathers ultimately arrived at a suitable bargain between Elsie and Walter. In this close-knit community, it would be necessary for Martin to secure a good Jewish wife for his son and even more important for Oskar to secure a productive son for his daughter.

Jewish artifacts and art pieces on display in the photographs of the Roth and Zwieback homes reflected their station in Austrian Jewish society. As part of their cultural and religious lives, they likely celebrated the High Holy days as well as the Passover Sader. Neither family adhered strictly to religious observance or practices. Later in life, the Roths remained conservative and observant of their traditions. Unfortunately, fewer details in this regard are known about the Zwiebacks, as most perished before the liberation of Europe. The families Jewish circles were likely social, or trade related. Eva described her family as "traditionalists," who observed the Jewish holidays and customs. Regardless of the entreaties, Walter and Elsie met and came to know one another and on December 25, 1930, they stood under a Chuppah and became husband and wife.

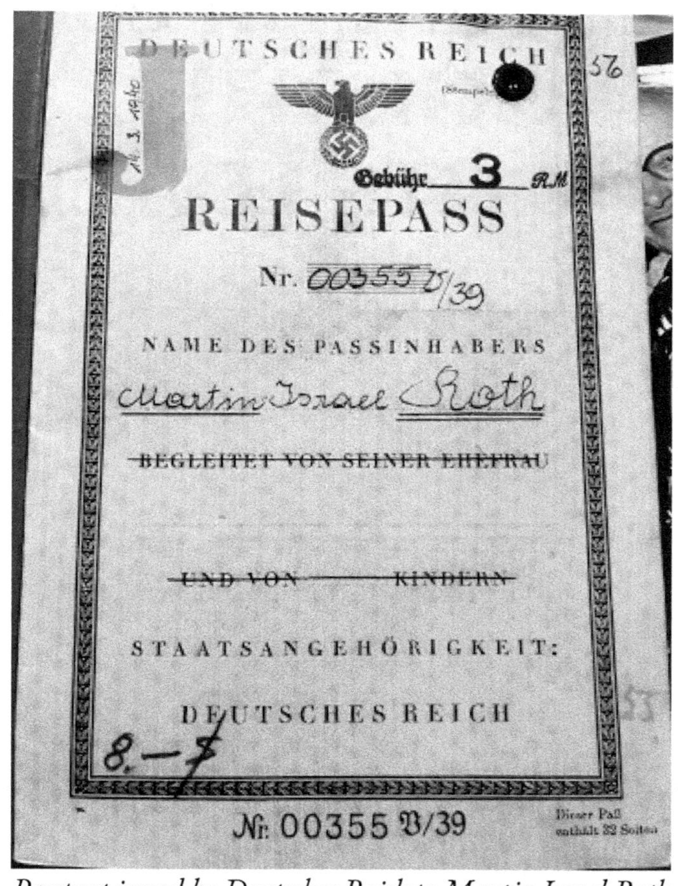

DEUTSCHES REICH

Gebühr 3 RM

REISEPASS

Nr. 00355 V/39

NAME DES PASSINHABERS

Martin Israel Roth

~~BEGLEITET VON SEINER EHEFRAU~~

~~UND VON KINDERN~~

STAATSANGEHÖRIGKEIT:

DEUTSCHES REICH

Nr. 00355 V/39

Dieser Paß enthält 32 Seiten

Passport issued by Deutsches Reich to Martin Israel Roth

The Little Colonel Wants it All

"It is worse to be evil than to do evil."
-ETHICS, Dietrich Bonhoeffer

On March 22, 1933, Walter and Elsie welcomed their daughter, Eva Marion, into their home under the shadow of a disaffected, Austrian colonel by the name of Adolf Hitler. With great hubris, he planned to conquer Europe, perhaps the world. A little less than a month before Eva's birth, the Reichstag (German Parliament building in

Berlin) was set on fire. The Roths busy with the approach of Eva's birth, overlooked this piece of news as many Austrians did. This event, however, would change the lives of the populace of Europe and the rest of the world. A summary of the political atmosphere of the moment is essential to set the stage for all that followed and led to the Roth's precipitous search for a route out of Austria and ultimately Europe.

Looking back, it is difficult to understand how Hitler, a penniless, ill-bred, and poorly educated braggart, rose to a position of prominence and power. Against all logic, he gathered support from many segments of German society. His message and ideas resonated among those who feared the communist and despised the armistice and its humiliating terms. Those disenchanted with the aristocracy, the elitist military ranks, and the Kaiser likewise found Hitler appealing.

A decade earlier, Hitler sought to organize the *Beer Hall* putsch (military takeover) in Munich. The attempt failed and antagonized the political establishment in the process. As a result, in 1923, the authorities moved to silence him. Hitler was charged with treason for trying to overthrow the Reich and received a lengthy prison term.

The colonel used his time in prison to put his plan to paper. His comfortable confinement in the Landsberg fortress provided access to newspapers, books, and a writing table. There, he wrote a two-volume book of insignificant literary value titled, *Mein Kampf* ("My Struggle") which he published in 1924. Its writings mapped out Hitler's strategy for changing the face of the world. Hitler's book formulated the thesis of the "Jewish Menace". As part of his theory, he manufactured the great Jewish conspiracy for world domination. Hitler blamed Germany's problems on the Jews and the communists.

Many in Austria and Germany overlooked *Mein Kampf*, its ultra-nationalistic fervor, its themes, and its ideology. But these provided the spark that led to the formation of the Nationalist Socialist Party. Hitler promised unity, dignity, and economic prosperity and while these promises resonated with a segment of the population the fulfillment of such promises lacked credulity. Hitler's demeanor revealed no social graces or refinement. He was rather a bombast with a proclivity for fiery temperamental outbursts. He lacked handsome or appealing features, social relations, or connections with the aristocracy and military hierarchy, yet his rhetoric filled the beer halls. Although he surrounded himself with those who held political and military ambitions, Hitler's lone confidant appears to have been a German American piano player and short-lived "friend," Ernst Hanfstaengl (nicknamed, "*Putzi*").

Despite overwhelming odds, the message of a man with limited artistic or literary skill, a passion for wolves, and a disdain for Jews, gained traction. In university circles and among the student fraternities, his ideology resonated. These fraternity groups, which mostly met in secret espoused nationalism and racism. What started as a call to unity and prosperity fueled the seeds of hatred and a revolution.

Hitler's Nationalist Socialist Party (later known as, the Nazi Party), found broad support over a decade. In January 1933, Hitler became German Chancellor through appointment by Germany's President, Paul von Hindenburg, and the compromise appointment resulted in a power share with Vice-Chancellor Franz von Papen.

Following Hitler's ascension, the Dutch "anarchists" Marinus Van der Lubbe single handedly burnt and severely damaged Germany's seat of power, the Reichstag. It is unclear who set the fire; nevertheless, Hitler's "Spin Doctor," Joseph Goebbels, promoted the theory that the communists set the fire. The fire in turn became the pretext to eliminate political opposition allowing the Nazi Party to strengthen. In 1933, the Nazi party coalesced and implemented a broadly worded Reichstag Fire decree and its enabling statutes. This decree provided for the suspension of *habeas corpus* (unlawful, indefinite imprisonment) among other civil rights. Furthermore, these laws fomented fear and hatred among the German population leading to the boycott and looting of Jewish businesses. Emboldened by the notable indifference of the broader population, the party and its members targeted Jews and other minority groups and burnt books deemed un-German.

In an indiscriminate manner, Austria took its lead from Germany and began to marginalize and oust Jewish professionals, business owners, and tradesmen from their established positions in society. Still, many Austrian Jews, including many of Walter and Elsie's elders, shut their eyes to the threat of complete obliteration. The optimists hoped outside forces would contain the threats. Pragmatist may have concluded that economic and cultural imperatives created barriers they could not overcome. Walter and Elsie, however, began to have discussions about their future and where they might live as the increasingly repressive environment for Jews living in Austria grew. Their foresight may have saved their lives.

While Hitler consolidated power in Austria and elsewhere, another Austrian, a lawyer named Theodore Herzl, gave lectures in Vienna where he promoted the concept of Zionism. In Austria and Vienna, he spoke mostly to Jewish intellectuals promoting the idea of a Jewish homeland in Palestine (ancient Biblical Judea). Palestine seemed an idealistic dream rather than a viable and practical resettlement plan, yet Herzl's ideas were likely the source of debate in synagogues across Western Europe. For antisemites, the prospect that Jews would leave Europe for a Middle Eastern wasteland seemed delightful and even encouraged. For city-dwelling Jews, Palestine held no appeal. At a time when nomadic Arabs overran Palestine, the prospects for this desert land seemed bleak. A large segment in Palestine lived in *wadis* and marshlands that barely produced fruit for meagre incomes. Only someone like Herzl could dare dream that this land would become the thriving and modern State of Israel in less than 50 years.

Jewish immigration to Palestine gained popularity in 1917 after Great Britain issued the Balfour declaration. The declaration supported the establishment of a "national home for the Jewish People." The declaration gave legitimacy to Herzl's Zionist movement but created significant blowback in Palestine. The declaration overlooked the interests of the Christians and Muslims making up most of the population of Palestine at the time. Amidst such tensions, Herzl left Europe with only a trickle of European Jews willing to champion the cause for a Jewish homeland in Palestine.

The rapid ascent to power by Adolph Hitler and his ability to consolidate power among seemingly different politicians and social economic groups caught Austria and most of Europe by surprise. Walter and Elsie were perceptive and courageous in their willingness to abandon their parents' homeland and all that they knew to pursue an unknown future overflowing with danger along the way.

The Calderon Tips

"Those who cannot remember the past are condemned to repeat it." George Santayana, The Life of Reason (1905).

The Jewish community in Vienna gradually came to grips with the reality of Hitler's annexation of their homeland. Some rabbis and community leaders responded by promoting emigration to South America, Australia, and Africa. After the annexation, the Austrian Jewish cultural center began offering classes in rudimentary Spanish and lessons on South American geography and culture. Walter Roth's family business had started to wane, and the day-to-day responsibilities of providing for his family filled his days. In retrospect, it's understandable that only a few had the foresight to see what lay ahead.

The decade preceding the war were taken up with the haberdashery and caring for Elsie and in the later days Walter's young daughter. As an apprentice to his dad and father-in-law's business, Walter needed to focus on showing himself approved before his elders. Nothing suggests he cared much for the politics of the day. Walter, a secular Jew, did not obediently fall back on the rabbinate for guidance or instructions. He observed the holidays and traditions with his family, and that seemed to suit him well.

After Germany's annexation of Sudetenland and Austria, the National Socialists continued to strengthen, consolidate power, and put laws in place to rein in the Jews. Laws emerged limiting the schools which Jewish children could attend, other laws restricted travel, professions, and places in which to socialize or assemble. Since Eva had not yet reached school age and Walter worked for his father, the first set of anti-Jewish laws had limited impact on their lives. The first critical test came when the Nazis ordered that his father's store display a sign, designating it as a Jewish shop. This made the store a target for antisemites seeking to harm Jews and succeeded in scaring most customers.

Antisemitic laws put in place compelled Walter and Elsie's parents to consider how to live the "new life" as a Jew. They only knew one home - Austria. They could not contend with the reality that, as Jews, they would have to leave "their" country. Many family discussions and arguments ensued. They believed they were part of the Austrian Republic as much as Walter and Elsie's parents were the last generation of the Austro-Hungarian Empire. In discussions, Walter and Elsie gave careful and cautious consideration to where refuge may lie until the war passed over. Two likely places emerged: Czechoslovakia (presently the Czech Republic and Slovakia) and Yugoslavia (after the Yugoslav wars throughout the 1990s the countries of Slovenia, Croatia, Macedonia, Bosnia-Herzegovina, Serbia, and Montenegro make up the former Yugoslavia). Both were places where the Roths and the Zwiebacks had friends and family relations as their grandparents had settled in Austria after leaving their ancestral homes in Hungary, Yugoslavia, and Czechoslovakia.

As the Roths cautiously laid out their departure plans, laws changed again. New laws enacted by the new government dictated cumbersome procedures. Those wanting to emigrate would need to apply for an exit permit through their local town's municipal office. As part of the permit application, applicants needed a good character certificate, as well as a certificate of good health. These requirements brought about anxiety. They were intended to humiliate, hinder and delay those desiring to flee the country.

There were additional decrees that required an inventory of all the applicant's assets with further disclosure of assets exceeding 5,000 Reichsmarks (around $2000 in US dollars, an equivalent of $34,000 in 2018). Those seeking to leave the country needed to pay an exit permit fee. To complement the decrees, a new Nazi bureaucracy, the *Vermogensverkehrstelle* (Asset Transfers Office) of the *Ministerium fur Handel und Verkehr*, (Ministry of Transportation and Commerce) sprung up three weeks later to oversee and track the transfer of Jewish assets into Aryan hands. These laws had the singular objective of displacing and marginalizing Jews socially and economically. Individuals seeking exit permits and travel documents were increasingly targeted by groups opposed to their presence in Vienna and other areas of Austria. These laws were unsettling to most, particularly those with assets and high social status. The Roths had immediate and practical concerns. If they surrendered all the assets upon declaring their intent to depart, they would have nothing of value to live on upon leaving the country.

Once the Roth's determined to flee Austria they considered all that must be set aside: clothes, non-perishable food, and other necessities. Walter quietly began to store up what he could and asked Elsie to hoard dry goods and all manner of necessaries. These would be in great demand once war broke out or if they were kept from leaving. Those not immediately thinking of leaving their beloved Austria, his parents, and Elsie's parents probably secreted some of their jewelry, cash, and goods to use to support their children's journey. These goods could be for immediate sale and disposition while others were to be kept for use elsewhere as the need arose. The plans for those leaving were fluid. This was new territory where no one could project how much would be enough. Some felt secure in the belief that British and Americans had cause to prevent another great war and would come to the aid of the continent. However, the cautious perceived the present threat compelled action until the menacing armies were contained or surrendered. Few could envision that the war would engulf most of the world and destroy the life they knew during five brutal and interminable years.

Walter and Elsie likely spent many sleepless nights in the days and weeks that followed pondering "what ifs." They considered secretly leaving through the very porous border with Czechoslovakia, but this option raised other concerns. Could they enter Czechoslovakia without an exit permit and blend into the towns or villages in the periphery of Brno? Perhaps Walter could work within the Jewish community until the war ended? Surely, there would always be a need for clothing and a tailor's craft. How would he move about without proper identity documents? There were many traveling and working with forged documents those days, but the consequences if caught were unacceptable to a father with a young family. They thought about Yugoslavia where their presence could be concealed in a rural or remote village. If they succeeded in slipping into Yugoslavia, what could Walter do to support his family? He did not know how to bake, farm, or tend to animals, and there would be little need for fine garments in small towns during wartime. After much debate, Walter concluded their presence would be more noticeable in a small town even if the Jewish community of such towns provided him and his family shelter.

As the idea of leaving Austria took shape, Walter and Elsie experienced a mixture of fear and apprehension that consumed their days. Their parents had not yet come to this point. While fearful about the swift transformation of their county, they, like many Jews in the late 1930s, still had their home and family. They echoed the sentiments of those of their generation adhering to the false sense of security that the world would come to the aid of a vulnerable, defenseless Jewish populace.

Most Austrian jews seeking to leave soon learned that none, but a trickle could enter the United States embassy. Even those fortunate to enter the inner sanctum of the embassy walked out without the elusive visa. Each day, the situation in Vienna continued to deteriorate. Standing in line outside an embassy subjected those waiting to taunt and jeers and, at times injury from thrown rocks and bottles. Walter decided to pursue a visa from another country, perhaps in South America. Walter knew they could not stay in Austria much longer where he no longer felt safe to take Eva to the park near their home. Elsie, in fear, stayed home except for essential trips to the butcher or market. Synagogues were closing, and people were hoarding anything they could salvage expecting the borders to close around them at any moment. In this time of uncertainty, most were left to conjecture. The newspapers and radio were unreliable, and most credible news spread by word of mouth among those in the Jewish community.

Just as Walter reached the point of despair and discouragement, he started a conversation with a man who, like him, hoped to get a visa for himself and his family. They had joined each other in the queue outside one embassy on several occasions and talked of possibilities for departure.

On a certain morning, the man approached with great secrecy as Walter stood in line. He shared that he had heard that a small and relatively obscure country in South or Central America was giving out visas. He had heard through his friends that many had succeeded in obtaining a visa to Cuba with the hope that entry to Cuba might forge a pathway to the United States. While this possibility appeared enticing, he failed to obtain any visa while in Vienna.

Disenchanted by his failure to obtain a permit to leave the country, Walter thought they could reach the Czech border before it closed. His family could travel on foot to Brno and then try to find a way out of the continent through Prague. With the help of Walter's father and step-mother, they connected with relatives who would give him and his family shelter until they could safely leave Prague. For the border crossing to be successful, he needed a plan that required a little luck and a clear path. Elsie would need to prepare Eva for travel through dense brush and coax her to stay quiet and out of sight until they could get across.

Walter and Elsie decided on the night of the new moon. They hoped that, as in the Sabbath eve song, *Adon Olam,* G-d would be a light and refuge to guide the family and cross through farmlands and forests into Czechoslovakia. They left their home on foot before dawn. Their plan resembled that of others in the Jewish community, but success would prove difficult. The Czech border guards were on the lookout for Jews trying to cross the border, and, sure enough, they were spotted by Austrian guards who intercepted them at the border. The family froze in fear. They were forcibly escorted to a guardhouse where they were kept for a few hours before being released back to Vienna. As they headed back Eva became ill which Elsie attributed to an excess of wild strawberries along the way. The fall and early frost had not yet damaged the harvest. Blessedly, there were no arrests that night, just threats, warnings, and insults.

A shaken Walter and his family returned to their home in Vienna that night. They were fearful the Austrian authorities would come for them and drag them off to the police station or seek to extort a bribe in exchange for their silence. If they tried to leave again, they would need to obtain exit permits. This would be costly and result in a dangerous delay and the possible forfeiture of their savings. As they contemplated their next steps life for Viennese Jews became more difficult. Despite obstacles, their more persistent friends and neighbors found ways to leave. Walter's father, Martin, had given up on the city he loved dearly, now merely a shadow of its resplendent and cheerful past, and in a precipitous move closed his business. Martin then turned his sights to his family that still remained in a small town in Yugoslavia.

With more caution and precision, Walter and Elsie began a new plan to escape. After their failed attempt, they regained courage, determined to make their departure anew. This time, they retained an experienced guide to meet them in the outskirts of Vienna. To avoid attention, as the sun began to creep up on the horizon, the three Roths walked out of their home with only a small bag in hand. They left their vehicle parked in the front door of their apartment building and purposely drew open the shades to suggest at most a short-day trip. They walked several kilometers before they met up with their guide. Late that night, they began a new trek into Czechoslovakia. This time, however, the guide knew the landscape, leading them in a circuitous manner to avoid guards and open areas. This approach allowed them to reach what the guide knew to be the least guarded section of the border. Undetected, they crossed the border and continued their walk under the shelter of darkness through damp fallen leaves, brush and pastureland. The next day, damp, exhausted and famished, they reached family near Brno.

Within days of their departure, the Nationalist Socialists unleashed a night of terror in Vienna. The rabble, undeterred by local authorities, looted or burnt scores of

Jewish homes and businesses. They looted but did not burn the Turner Synagogue adjacent to Martin's apartment. This synagogue was designed and constructed in the mid 1800s to look like a residential building and may have confused the looters as to the nature of the structure. This event no doubt precipitated Martin and Frieda's (Martin's second wife) to consider leaving their beloved Vienna.

The Roths joyfully and thankful to have arrived in Walter's uncle's home in Brno. New worries arose, however, after Eva spiked a fever on the journey. Eva, delicate and barely five years of age, had been exposed to the cold and damp air overnight. Her poor health presented a new challenge. The Roths had crossed the border but now grappled with an unknown illness in an unfamiliar place. At first, Elsie thought the fever could be from a cold. When it would not subside, they feared it could be something more serious. Eva's health continued to deteriorate, requiring a doctor. He quickly diagnosed the condition as diphtheria. Their journey would need to pause.

Germany would invade Czechoslovakia in just a few months, and medicines were already in short supply. With the help of others in the community, Walter and Elsie heeded the doctor's orders obtained what was available, likely camphor and aspirin. Although, penicillin would have been an ideal treatment, it was not widely available in the late 1930s. The remedies applied coupled with cold compresses and lots of *haldzn* (hugs) from Elsie and Walter brought about recovery. After much prayer, G-d's hand relented, but they would have to remain in this place for a few weeks until Eva grew stronger, and they could map out their route west.

Eva finally recovered from diphtheria that had lasted a few weeks. She appeared frail but strong enough to travel. The Roths headed for Prague with a reinvigorated Eva, while Hitler moved to annex the northern areas of Czechoslovakia. The annexation arose following the Munich Agreement, an attempt at appeasement, signed by the Nazis, Fascist and the United Kingdom and France on September 30th, 1938. The agreement allowed the annexation by Hitler of an area inhabited by mostly ethnic Germans and opened the door to the invasion of the rest of Czechoslovakia and led to the partition of various parts of Czechoslovakia into various neighboring countries. Many of the 24,000 Jews living in Sudetenland prior to the annexation attempted to leave before being deported or detained. Many of them headed for Prague at the same time the Roths sought safe harbor with their relatives in Prague.

Prague would not be fully invaded and occupied by German troops until March 1939. During the six months following the annexation of the Sudetenland the Nazis consolidated their control throughout Czechoslovakia and ultimately Prague. The Czech capital was a large thriving European urban center with a large Jewish population. Between 100,000 to 120,000 Jews lived in Czechoslovakia prior to Germany's occupation. Most of those resided in the Jewish Quarter in Prague, flanked by the Vltava River and the Old Town Square. Prior to Nazi occupation, the Jewish Quarter contained six synagogue and its own cemetery dating back to the 1400s. As the Germans consolidated their power in Northern Czechoslovakia, much of its Jewish population sought shelter in Prague's Jewish Quarter. It was in this Quarter that the Roths would plan their departure out of Europe.

The winter months in Prague were fruitful. While the daily visits to the United States Consulate failed to produce a visa, other efforts would be successful. The Roths obtained Czech passports on October 27, 1938, which did not bear the "J" stamped on the Austrian passports issued by the Nazis in Vienna. This crucial detail may have been the catalyst that allowed their movement out of Czechoslovakia. With the support of their relatives in Austria and Czechoslovakia and a tip from their aunt Gretel, Walter's sister, a pathway emerged. They learned that a country in South America might be selling visas to prospective immigrants. They trusted in Gretel who, like them, sought to immigrate. With her tip in hand, Walter went on to procure visas, no matter their provenance. As providence would have it, he reached the consulate of the República Oriental del Uruguay and met with success. Walter and Elsie knew little about Uruguay, and neither did their uncle. They knew some beef products in Vienna came from the Southern Cone, and they had also seen sheepskin or leather jackets from Uruguay in one of the stores near Needastreetsky Street.

Despite their ignorance about their destination or their future, the Roths now perceived a ray of hope on their horizon. With visas in hand, they would need to secure transportation to this country which offered an opportunity to escape the wrath that would be unleashed in Europe. Any hesitation would have doomed them to the fate of most Jews living in Prague. Of approximately 125,000 Jews identified in March 1939, only 88,000 remained in October of 1941. More than half of those lived in Prague, the remaining in Bohemia and Moravia. Those in Moravia were transferred to Theresienstadt (Terezin) camp and ghetto 30 miles north of Prague. Between 1941 and 1942 most Jews in the camp were deported to death camps. Only 15,000 Jews would be liberated at the end of the war.

Walter and Elsie found it difficult to contemplate departure from the only world they knew. They were apprehensive about the challenges they would encounter on the next leg of their journey. While in Czechoslovakia, they grew close to many of their relatives. They would miss them and perhaps never see them again. Their hearts also pined for their family and friends in Austria. While in Prague, Elsie met her cousin, Lilla Svarcz Drexler. Lilla lived in Prague with her husband, Janos, a Hungarian Jew. As they said their good-byes, they sensed these might be permanent and final embraces. They found it particularly difficult to part from Gretel, who had the foresight to direct them to the consulate that provided their visas. Gretel would leave for London ahead of them. Sometime later, she married Barnes, an Austrian, and settled in Australia where they raised several children and lived to enjoy many grandchildren.

In Prague, the Roths, with the help of their family and a network of Jewish confidants, formulated a plan to reach South America. They would travel to the port of Antwerp, Belgium, one of the last remaining departure points still open to Jewish refugees. Their uncles with contacts in Belgium identified a ship that would make the crossing to South America and take passengers, but the Roths had a limited window by which to reach the port. They also needed a pretext for the family to travel from Prague to Belgium. They considered contriving a trip for medical care for Eva who remained sickly after recovering from her bout with diphtheria as well. The distance from Prague to Brussels spanned approximately 600 miles. Meandering by train mostly through the countryside at a pretty good clip and stopping in cities along the way would run overnight. Once in Brussels, they would need to find transport to the port of Antwerp about 50 miles away. The danger laid in the rail segment from Prague through Dresden and Frankfort, Germany where Nazis already considered Jews a pariah. If detained in Frankfort, there would be no return home.

Prague: Entrance to Jewish Quarter

Art Nouveau style architecture found in the Jewish Quarter

"A principal street in Jewish ghetto"

Oldest synagogue in Central Europe – Circa 13th Century

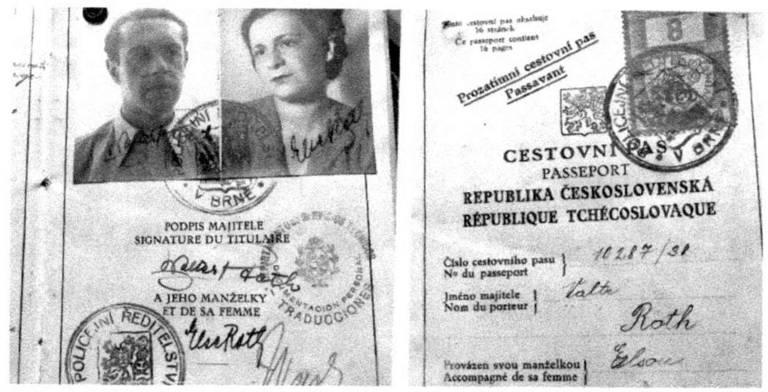

PODPIS MAJITELE
SIGNATURE DU TITULAIRE
A JEHO MANŽELKY
ET DE SA FEMME

Prozatímní cestovní pas
Passavant
CESTOVNÍ PAS
PASSEPORT
REPUBLIKA ČESKOSLOVENSKÁ
RÉPUBLIQUE TCHÉCOSLOVAQUE
Číslo cestovního pasu
N° du passeport
Jméno majitele
Nom du porteur
Roth
Provázen svou manželkou
Accompagné de sa femme

Republic of Czechoslovakia, Passport issues to Walter and Elsie Roth October 27, 1938

Consulado de la República O. del Uruguay
Brno (Checo-Eslovaquia) 10. II. 1939
Visto para su visación el presente pasaporte
No. 10287/38.
El Cónsul.

Entry stamp by Republica Oriental del Uruguay consulate on February 10, 1939

The MS Copacabana was neither captured nor sunk, and she spent the entire Second World War as a fast cargo ship between England and South America. A fast modern ship, she sailed without escort. She assisted during the evacuation of Antwerp on May 14, 1940.

On the MS Copacabana

Looking through Rose-Colored Glasses

Just as resources and patience were about to run out, Walter found the sought-after freighter with the help of the harbormaster. He approached the ship and its captain with some degree of apprehension. In this instance, his fears were unfounded. The captain behaved professionally and permitted him and his family, as well as a group of approximately two dozen individuals, to embark without incident.

After weeks of uncertainty, the Roths had a date of departure. Elsie methodically prepared for the lengthy Atlantic crossing. Eva excitedly looked upon the next part of the journey --- yet another adventure. She had never been on a ship and looked forward to moving out of her cold cramped environment with no friends or places to play. Elsie and Walter were relieved but tremulous. Eva had been sick during the three weeks they spent in Antwerp. They would now sail for several weeks through turbulent and dangerous waters that were filled with commercial ships as well as armed ships on patrol ready to engage any vessel perceived hostile. They did not know the exact length of the Atlantic crossing or who would share the ship with them. They also feared Uruguay might not honor their visas or receive them into their country. The Roths took an unimaginable leap of faith.

At first light on a cold spring morning, the Roths, warmly clothed with little baggage and all their concealed treasures, headed to the designated pier and slip to board their ship. Guards were on the gangplanks checking passports and visas. As they approached the dock checkpoints, they saw other families appearing to head in the direction of the *Copacabana*. As they boarded, they learned that the passengers would be traveling together: all Jews, all fleeing the same demon. At least a dozen of those boarding sought to make Uruguay their new home. Among those onboard the ship was Irene Rosenberg, a woman with whom Eva would connect 20 years later and forge a lifelong friendship.

The freighter provided cabins below deck. These served as their tight quarters during more than two months. To their surprise, the ship, a newer class mixed liner commissioned in 1937, provided some unexpected comforts.

Eva, the only child aboard the ship, was just six years of age when she boarded. At the outset of the trip, her presence presented a challenge to Elsie and Walter, as well as to those not used to a precocious child. Immediately upon setting sail, Eva became ill, with a lingering cold and intermittent fever. The damp, sea breeze, close quarters, and poor diet further compromised her health. After passing through some difficult days, by G-d's grace, Eva rebounded and succeeded in endearing herself to the captain and crew. At this young age, she loved to sing in Czech and German. She also spoke some English words which her mom taught her in anticipation of their departure from Austria. Most on board suffered from the interminable rocking of the ship and the dreariness of their surroundings. Luckily, one crewman or another, amused by the young girl, frequently invited Eva on deck. As the days passed, Eva adapted to the sea and looked strong and in good health as they approached the coast of South America. After several weeks with musty cabin smell and the dampness of the ocean filling the air, the coast of South America brought bright sun and warm breezes.

Gradually, early morning clouds and misty fog uncovered Rio de Janeiro harbor in the heart of the steamy Brazilian tropics. The backdrop revealed jagged mountains, lush vegetation, and unusual land formations. The passengers now shared a bond, and strong friendships were forming. When the freighter reached the harbor, the captain permitted passengers to come on deck, but they could not debark. Those bound for Uruguay had "tourist visas" for Uruguay, but no permits to enter Brazil. As the passengers peered onto the deck, the blinding, scorching heat of the sun overwhelmed them. They had crossed the equator, and nothing in Southern Europe would have compared to Rio and the intensity of its heat and humidity.

Eva seemed eager and excited for her adventure to continue. All at once, she experienced an explosion of colorful sights and sounds. The rhythmic utterance of Portuguese, brightly colored dresses, dark skins, unfamiliar odors, and vibrating sounds emerging from drums, guitars, and unusual musical instruments. There were vendors everywhere barefooted pushing carts, luring customers with persistent rhythmic chants. All these sounds came from the docks only a few steps away. At a distance, she spotted hills and mountains, tall trees, houses, and strange animals.

Nothing looked like anything she had seen back in Europe. A pale, green-eyed, red head, she stood out before these tanned people of the tropics. She wished and prayed her impatience, or excitement would catch the attention of someone from the crew. As the crew started to ready for shore leave, the captain arranged for Eva to leave the ship with one of his crew members and tour the bustling city. To the crew, Eva became their "talisman," a lucky charm. Comfortable and warm to this young child, with her singing and incessant talking, they took her touring. To her last days, Eva retained a now faded black and white photo taken of her with some crewmembers overlooking the mountain peak, Corcovado (meaning, "Hunchback"). This narrow summit in Rio de Janeiro with its statute of Christ the Redeemer has kept watch over the city since the early 1930s.

Back on board, Eva had enough excitement and sensory overload to keep her going for a while. The ship stayed in Rio loading cargo for a few days before heading south towards Montevideo, the capital of the small southern cone country of Uruguay that is flanked by Brazil and Argentina north and south. As the ship drew closer to the port, the mood below deck grew in excitement, but also concern. No one felt secure with the validity of their "tourist visas," and these fears were well grounded. For the Roths and likely some of the other passengers, other challenges loomed. How would they support themselves once in Uruguay? How would they communicate, find housing, and move about? The Roths did not speak a modicum of Spanish, although Elsie spoke French, English, German and Yiddish.

They arrived at Montevideo harbor but quickly learned they could not disembark. Out beyond the Sarandi jetty, the Uruguayan immigration authorities boarded the ship for an initial inspection. Upon examination of the passengers' papers, they determined none of the "tourists" had purchased return tickets to their homeland. The authorities raised questions about the legitimacy of their documents and status as "tourists." Knowing the threat if returned to Europe, a passenger managed to send a message out to Jewish groups in Montevideo. He hoped they might intercede on the passengers' behalf but knew it would be some time before a response could be received. Since the ship could not afford to remain idle in Montevideo, the captain determined to go back up to Buenos Aires and secure additional cargo. Meanwhile the authorities would sort out the fate of his passengers. For Eva, the trip to Buenos Aires brought more shore leave and discovery. The ship's crew pitied her and took her on excursions while her parents and other passengers remained virtual prisoners on board the ship for two weeks.

The ship docked in Buenos Aires, replenished provisions, took on additional cargo, and then turned back towards Montevideo on its return course back to Europe. The passengers were dreading the next days of their journey. If their Jewish brethren could not negotiate the passengers' entry into Uruguay, the captain would have to return to Antwerp with its passengers. By the early months of 1939 the German military maintained an occupying force in Belgium, a full-scale invasion just a few months away. This conjured up visions of confinement or death in Europe as Germany threatened to control a greater part of the continent. If they were ever to pray, this would be the time. The G-d who spared the Israelites in the desert and carried them across the Red Sea would neither leave them nor forsake them. He would be their beacon of light into Montevideo.

On May 11, 1939, the *Copacabana* and its weary passengers once again reached Montevideo, but the Uruguayan Ministry of the Interior did not allow her to enter the harbor. The harbor pilots commandeered the ship to the Sarandi jetty, at the mouth of the harbor, where Mr. Israelson of the Uruguayan immigration services met the now stateless "tourists." He arranged for the passengers to come on shore on several small dinghies, presumably for "some months," until the authorities reached a resolution on the passengers' immigration status. The tourists were now refugees. Mr. Israelson helped these passengers as well as other Jews who sought refuge in Uruguay. Their belongings miraculously made it to the port, and they were now walking on a cloud, reassured that they were safe and in a neutral country.

The early days in Montevideo were weary, different, exciting, and confusing. Upon reaching the port complex, the Roths and their shipmates were escorted off the ship to experience the endless maze of Uruguayan bureaucracy. After hours of questions and triplicate forms on carbon paper in front of interpreters they barely understood, the Uruguayan authorities released the group. For the first year of their stay in Montevideo, Walter would be required to report to the police station every day. Their fates were in the hands of Jewish relief agencies, now their sponsors and facilitators. They would address their immediate needs for housing, food, clothing, and work.

If the group did not know how blessed they were to have been welcomed in Montevideo, those in the Jewish community and agencies were painfully aware of the precariousness of their situation. On May 10th, after the group gained permission to enter Montevideo, a much larger group, with equally questionable visas, left Hamburg for Cuba. In that instance, 931 passengers sailed on the *SS St. Louis* with tourist visas that provided for provisional settlement in Cuba until they could enter the United States under Cuba's immigration quota. Due to a shift in political power in Cuba and pressure exerted by German propaganda machine, debarking in Cuba became impossible. Initially, only 22 of the *St. Louis* passengers entered Cuba after paying a surcharge of US$500 per passenger to buy their entry into the country. The rest were left in limbo after the Cuban authorities rescinded the passenger's visas. Numerous charitable and philanthropic agencies made efforts to obtain refuge for the remaining passengers in other Caribbean Island nations. Through the intercession of the United States, another six passengers obtained last-minute entry. Ultimately, no country took in the remaining Jews of the *St. Louis* and the ship with its passengers returned to Europe by way of Antwerp under the tenuous protection of the Belgians, Dutch, and French. Through the records of the United States Holocaust Memorial Museum in Washington D.C., it is known that of those that returned, 80 of them made it to the United States before 1941, 200 died in the Holocaust and about 365 survived the war.

The Graf Spee

Montevideo Comes to Life

The first glimpse of Montevideo looked nothing like the sophisticated capitals of Vienna or even Prague. Montevideo appeared smaller and less urban than most European capitals, but they found the air cleaner and the streets less congested. They encountered a more provincial city, at times exceedingly conservative. To their surprise and amusement, women could not wear slacks in public, yet men could step out of their homes in pajamas on Sundays to listen to a soccer match on the radio. As the Viennese loved their cinnamon coffee, the Uruguayans had a national passion for *mate* (yerba mate), a bitter tea often sipped through an ornamental metal or silver straw with a filter inserted into a gourd. As they settled into this country, they learned that drinking *mate* is a cultural ritual as much as a thirst-quenching beverage.

The first immediate problem for Walter and Elsie became communication. Neither of them could speak Spanish, and most transactions had to be done through an interpreter. Soon after arriving, representatives from various Jewish organizations offered to assist the new Uruguayan refugees. These would have included, La Jewsektzia and Yidishim Kultem Oiz, together with Banco Israelita. These agencies raised funds for Austrian refugees entering Uruguay. With their assistance, the Roths were provided a new third-floor apartment in a mid-rise building at 25 de mayo, 371, Apartment 18, in the Ciudad Vieja section of Montevideo, just a few blocks from the western entrance to the port. They would live there for many years, and Eva would stay there until age 14.

A hodgepodge of port workers and European Jews, including recent arrivals, resided at 25 de mayo, a centrally located building in a crowded and less affluent section of the city. They settled there, made friends, and soon learned to understand the language as much as the culture. The family quickly developed an appetite for meats and sausages roasted in wood-burning stoves, piping hot empanadas, and the ritual of sipping *mate*. Despite the new flavors, the buildings still poured out the mouth-watering smells of fresh baked Challah on a Sabbath eve together with that of sweets and kosher Ashkenazi favorites. In a very short time, these new dwellers adapted to their neighborhoods and circumstances. Likewise, their diets and lifestyles would embrace the new continent with its different climate, inverted seasons, and greater informality among their relations. The friendships made while on the journey would become their initial social circle and companions to cafes and marketplaces.

Much of the money and valuables the Roths brought out of Vienna would be carefully managed until they could find a new income stream. The burden to find employment with haste fell to Walter. Similarly to other Jews who came from large European cities, Walter knew the garment industry. This served as a marketable skill in a country with an expansive wool industry. As with new immigrants and refugees in urban centers throughout North and South America, Walter possessed skills, motivation, tenacity, and creativity. These traits allowed him and other like-minded Jews to thrive.

To the Roths benefit, Uruguay's economy prospered from the war and its export of meat and wool products. The war also brought a demand for skilled workers. Walter, an exceptionally handsome man, called attention to himself in any surrounding; some said he looked like the Hollywood film actor, Rex Harrison. His countenance no doubt made him distinctive among the "orientales" in Montevideo. Despite his language limitations, he secured a job within his area of knowledge and experience within a few days. He became a merchandiser and sales representative at Frontex, a lingerie factory on Rivera Street in Montevideo, a short distance from their apartment building. Walter did well as lingerie distributor.

Elsie quickly became productive as well. Using her culinary skills, she started a type of luncheonette within her apartment building. Early each day, she awoke to prepare three plates for lunch to serve several immigrant families and charged each patron 10 to 12 cents per meal. This home enterprise helped with household expenses, but the toilsome effort took its toll on her. She became determined to seek other means of providing added income and fell back on the skills she learned in Europe. While in Vienna, Elsie learned to make artificial flower arrangements, and she valued the skill sufficiently to bring some of her tools with her on the ship. Shortly after settling in Uruguay, Elsie began to use her talents in making ornamental artificial flower arrangements for women's apparel and millinery shop.

Elsie's parents provided a good education for their daughter. In Vienna, she received a degree as a schoolteacher, although she never worked outside the home until coming to Uruguay. Her language skills coupled with her teaching preparation became a more significant source of income. Elsie, fluent in French and English, seldom needed to use her linguistic skills. In Montevideo, she used her language skills to tutor students and teach others those languages. Many years later, this would become the financial underpinnings of the Roths' livelihood in Paraguay.

After settling the issue of housing and employment, the Roths were determined to enroll Eva in school. Eva attended public school where her charming and jovial disposition attracted many friends. At first, Eva struggled with Spanish, but one of her new school mates, Clara, helped her to adjust. In the process, Clara became her close friend and confidant. Several years older than Eva, Clara was born in Uruguay to Jewish parents who emigrated from Poland, perhaps during the first World War. Clara deftly straddled both cultures. Although fluent in Spanish, Clara also spoke German. Whenever Eva experienced problems with understanding her teachers or classmates, Clara became the bridge. The challenges presented by the culture and language barriers did not discourage a determined and tenacious Eva. She believed herself to be a good student who could be one of the best in her class. In a brief timeframe, her nimble mind mastered Spanish, and her life soon became school and her relations with her schoolmates.

While gradually assimilating, the Roths were aware that being Jewish bound them to this new world of European immigrants. Their status in Uruguay remained provisionary for their first three years, and, during those initial years in Uruguay, their lives were inexorably tied to the war raging in Europe. There were constant reminders of the of war's horrific impact on European and dispersed Jews. Most Jews living in Uruguay had or knew of someone that had been left behind, trapped with fate and future unknown. Most Jews in Uruguay would not learn the reality of what transpired throughout Europe until the end of the war. Together with the rest of the world, newsreels and news headlines shockingly revealed the liberation of a remnant of tattered and emaciated Jews penned in concentration camps throughout the course of the war.

If the Roths had tried to put the war behind them after their arrival in Uruguay, they would not succeed. The apartment where they resided in the Old city laid proximate to the port's entrance; their building just a few blocks from the lighthouse on the Escollera de Sarandi and the Port of Montevideo. From the top of their apartment building, they could spot parts of the harbor where, on early mornings, they heard the ships' horns blearing as they navigated the port's entrance.

At the height of their first summer in Uruguay, the World War came into Montevideo. Before the Roths left Austria, they knew National Socialists had a plan in place for supremacy and world domination. Uruguay and its international press corps, as well as Great Britain vividly recount the clash between the British and the Nazis that played out in the mouth of the River Plate. Uruguayans were consumed by the events taking place at their front door.

Early in Germany's war plans, before the declaration of war, the Nazis deployed numerous ships, some of them to the South Atlantic. Ships were strategically positioned throughout merchant sea-lanes to be in place as belligerents upon declaration of war. The *Admiral Graf Spee* was among the German ships trolling the Atlantic, and this armored ship, nicknamed a "Pocket Battleship" by the British navy initially served in non-intervention patrols during the Spanish Civil war. When Europe declared war on September of 1939, the *Graf Spee* moved into action. At first, it raided allied merchant ships. However, by the end of September, its captain, Hans Langsdorff had orders to commence attacking ships in international waters. Over the ensuing three months, the *Graf Spee* raided and sunk nine ships. As a result, the destruction of the *Graf Spee* became a paramount priority for the allied navies. In October, the French and British navies formed eight groups with the objective of destroying the *Graf Spee*. Captain Langsdorff knew the allies would pursue his ship relentlessly. To avoid detection, he ordered the construction of dummy gun turrets and other visible structural changes to the ship to disguise its identity. By December 1939, Commodore Henry Harwood of the Royal Navy and three British ships had their sights on the *Graf Spee*. They converged on the mouth of the River Plate anticipating Langsdorff's next move.

Based on the sensitive shipping route information gathered by the *Graf Spee's* last raid, Langsdorff headed for the waters near Montevideo after sinking the freighter *Streonshahl* on December 7th. As the *Graf Spee* approached the Bay of Montevideo on December 13, she spotted the *HMS Exeter* and two smaller British ships. The *Graf Spee* opened fire and inflicted damage on the *Exeter* and the *Ajax*, but not without consequences. The three British ships, which included the *Achilles* retaliated and struck the *Graf Spee* multiple times causing significant damage to the ship. Langsdorff lost 36 of his men, and others crew sustained injuries, including Langsdorff himself. With the ship disabled, Langsdorff headed for shelter in Montevideo Harbor where he appealed under international law for entry into the port. The appeal would be granted for the distressed vessel to obtain care for its injured crew and to effectuate repairs to his ship sufficient to allow for its return to Germany.

As the ship appeared at the harbor's entrance, another battle brewed—this one of political nature. Uruguay had declared its neutrality, but its sympathies laid with the British. Adhering strictly to the Hague Convention, Uruguay allowed the *Graf Spee* to come into the harbor for 72 hours to make essential repairs. Large crowds gathered in Montevideo Harbor as the tug of war unfolded between the Germans, British, and Uruguayans. More than 20,000 onlookers camped out near the harbor to watch the ensuing showdown. Considering their proximity to the port, the Roths and their neighbors had a birds-eye view to the tension gripping the harbor.

The international press converged on Montevideo. The heat of summer and the significance of the moment created an intense atmosphere as the damaged ship approached the harbor. Upon mooring, the able crew carried out the wounded for medical treatment in Montevideo. The press reported that the dead were escorted out with full military honors and buried in Montevideo. Meanwhile, the fate of the *Graf Spee* remained uncertain. The British respected Uruguay's neutrality but remained at the ready to sink the ship should *Graf Spee* leave the harbor.

The drama ensued. On December 17, Captain Langsdorff ordered the destruction of the ship's sensitive equipment. The following day, he and a crew of forty remaining on board moved out to scuttle the ship. The aftermath left the British victorious, and its Commodore Harwood knighted and promoted to Rear Admiral. Captain Langstorff left Montevideo for Buenos Aires with the ship's surviving crew. Two days later, however, he committed suicide. Eva and her Jewish friends were likely among those who walked to the harbor to watch the sinking of the *Graf Spee*. In the early 1960s Uruguay erected a memorial marking the sinking of the *Graf Spee* in the port of Montevideo. The Roths and shipmates were now witnesses to Uruguay's imprint on the world stage of World War II. Eva's memory of the sinking of the *Graf Spee* remained with her throughout her life.

After the sinking of the *Graf Spee*, Uruguay returned to its staid way of life. Two worlds existed, however: One for the European immigrants, another for the nationals. For the immigrants, their focus remained firmly on the progression of the war in Europe. This issue fully absorbed the Jewish community (or the "colectividad" as Uruguayans referred to the Jewish community). Eva could not detach herself from the scourge of the war. During those years, Walter, Elsie, and their social circles engaged in social pursuits, the occasional game of cards, movies, and attendance at the local club. Invariably, however, most conversations turned to the war and those left behind.

Walter and Elsie did not forget those remaining in Austria. As news of the war unfolded, they followed the news of the debacle in Dunkirk, followed by the fall of Paris and bombings in London. These battles left them with little hope for the Jews of Europe. Those that managed to leave shared news of concentration camps for Jews and other marginalized groups. News from Europe trickled in giving accounts of squalid, inhumane camps. Such accounts were difficult to verify. With Jews scurrying from place to place and no means by which to track their movements, it became impossible to know who was hiding, captured, or remained in flight moving across borders. Eva could sense and empathize her family and friend's anxiety and despair. As a young girl she felt helpless.

In 1943, Walter and Elsie received the most unexpected but welcomed news. During the chaos and grim news filtering from all parts of Europe, they learned that Eva's paternal grandparents had succeeded in escaping deportation and detention. By 1942 the population of Jews remaining in Vienna had been reduced to 7,000, and Martin and Frieda were among the last Jews able to leave Austria. This miracle, as Eva described it, happened as her grandparents stood among a group assigned for transport (their arms already tattooed) to a work camp ("concentration camp"). As the assignment to assemble came, they negotiated for the relinquishment of their concealed assets in exchange for a visa and a first-class rail ticket from Vienna to Barcelona. The promised passage turned out to be a fraud. Instead of a passenger train, they were given passage in rail grain carts, segregated by gender and in less than sanitary or humane conditions. At the time, Eva's grandfather was in his 70s, and his wife, Frieda, in her 60s. Although Frieda was Martin's second wife, Eva, knew no other grandmother.

Upon learning of the incredible and most would say miraculous departure, Walter and Elsie took their savings and assets and pooled them towards bringing their parents to Uruguay. After Martin and Frieda arrived in Barcelona, they sought out a ship sailing for South America with the funds for passage which Walter and Elsie had made available to them. They made the crossing on a commercial carrier, arriving safely in Montevideo, thankful to be alive and with their family. They described their journey as difficult, describing the conditions on the ship as very poor.

Martin and Frieda, or Opi and Omi, as Eva endearingly called them in German, filled a void for Eva created by her parents who worked long hours to make headway in their new homeland. Opi and Omi moved into the same building as Walter and Elsie and secured their own space on the same building as Eva and her parents, just one floor below them. For Eva, their proximity allowed for spending time with her grandparents who brought nothing but joy and discovery to her life. Her grandfather, an intelligent and refined man, loved talking with her about his life experiences. He also showed interest in Eva's aspirations and day to day activities and provided the nurturing and attention she needed to blossom and assert herself in school and among her friends. Despite Opi's age and lack of understanding of Spanish upon arriving in Uruguay, he quickly gained employment. He became a distributor of notions for women's dress shops and continued working in this trade until he reached age 90.

Eva's grandmother stayed at home but like Elsie she had great culinary skills. With her pastry skills and experience Frieda proceeded to make refined delicious European tarts and cakes which she sold in the city. Eva delighted in her time with her and ultimately cared for her until her death.

Martin and Frieda Roth. - Montevideo, Uruguay

Opi and Omi developed their own social circle in Uruguay among their contemporaries. They were religiously observant, or at least much more traditional in their observances than their son. High Holiday observances as well as Passover were always celebrated in their home. In her grandparent's home, Eva learned much about Jewish holiday observances and traditions, and these formed the core of her Jewish foundation. Eva's sense of Jewishness grew stronger as the world war ended and the formation of the state of Israel became the rallying cry for diasporic Jews. Eva's grandparents instilled in her a lasting sense of pride in being Jewish. She clung to her appreciation for Judaism and its traditions despite marrying a nominal Catholic.

For Eva, life revolved around her school. The school days were long, and, in time, she forged strong bonds with a newer group of friends. Soon enough, her social world began to shift to sports and patriotic activities within the Asociacion Hebraica Macabi. This club allowed her to forge bonds with schoolmates and other young contemporaries in the Jewish community. The club included sports and social components. One segment emphasized team and competitive sports activities while the other focused on forming interactions and communal activities. Club members participated in camping and outdoor social gatherings and a foretaste of Kibbutz life. The activities served to complement a much greater objective in 1947 as Jews living in Palestine were embroiled in deadly skirmishes with the controlling British Authorities. By 1947, Jews living in Palestine could no longer tolerate British rule. The *Haganah*, the principal political Zionist organization, formed within Palestine with the support of ordinary Jews. Jews within and outside Palestine joined the *Haganah* fighting to create the State of Israel and its recognition by the United Nations.

Eva found the Macabi to be a warm and nurturing environment with endless opportunities for sports and entertainment for her age group. There she met Herbert Donner, also an Austrian Jew. Herbert served as one of her club leaders (*"Menahel"*). She also met and made another friend for life, Ruth (who would marry Dov Cohn). Although Ruth moved to the United States in the early 1950s, their correspondence and friendship remained uninterrupted throughout their lives. Eva's other great friends as she matured into womanhood were Greta and Clara.

In her teen years, Eva's focus, as well as the emphasis of club also shifted. Eva kept a journal of her activities within the club during the years 1946-1947. Her entries show an understanding and desire to grow in her Jewishness. Her journal includes references and photos of camp gatherings, outdoor cookouts, and club meetings. Reflecting the yearnings of a coming-of-age teen, she wrote poems about the joy of being Jewish and the quest for the formation of the state of Israel. She wrote about her studies within the club about Jewish leaders such as Theodore Herzl and Joseph Trumpeldor, who promoted Zionism. With sorrow and pain, she wrote about those who were lost in the struggle for Jewish independence. She wrote of men like Dov Bela Gruner, a member of the *Irgun*, who was executed by British authorities in 1947. After the formation of the State of Israel the club continued supporting its peers in *Eretz Ysrael*, ("the land of Israel") with some members moving to fight for the new Jewish state. This migration, or *Aliyah* (ascent) to the State of Israel has since become part of Jewish culture. The Club Deportivo Macabi maintains its recreational and athletic component with an emphasis on international friendship games, or the *Maccabiah*.

On November 29, 1947, Eva formed part of the crowd at the club which listened intently to witness the United Nations vote to approve the creation of the State of Israel. After the vote, the Macabi members celebrated with great exuberance. In 1948, the club and its members became staunch promoters of the formation of the State of Israel. It would take until May 1948 for the State of Israel to declare its independence from Great Britain. Upon the statehood declaration, Eva and the members of the club, and undoubtedly most of the Jews in Montevideo, converged on the intersection of 18 de Julio and the Plaza de Independencia in the center of the capital. In this historic gathering spot they waved flags, sang, danced the *hora*, and reveled in the independence of the Jewish state. Eva like the members of the club felt they were active "participants" in its creation. They had rallied behind something of their own.

Within hours of the declaration of independence, Israel would be thrust into war with her surrounding Arab neighbors. United Nations Resolution 181 adopted in

1947 called for partition of Palestine under the British Mandate. (presently Israel, the West Bank, The Gaza Strip and Jordan) into two states, one Jewish and one Arab, with international control over Jerusalem. The Arabs would not agree to the terms of the resolution, finding its terms inequitable. What began as skirmishes between Palestinian Arabs and Jews escalated upon the creation of the State of Israel on May 14, 1948. The day after the declaration of independence a multinational force from Egypt, Iraq, Lebanon, Jordan, and Syria attacked the State of Israel.

Many from Eva's Macabi group left for Israel. Some fought in the first or subsequent wars and incursions and several of them perished there. These events only served to solidify Eva's attachment to the State of Israel. Israel, not Austria, became her second homeland.

Walter and Elsie were content to see Eva growing and maturing into a sober minded young woman. They rejoiced in her interest in the club and her passion for the State of Israel. As such, they gave her latitude in her activities in the Macabis. Up until the age of 15, Eva spent most of her free time outside of school in club related activities. Eva regretted her parent's detachment from her day-to-day activities and friends. In retrospect, what she perceived as her parent's disinterest in her life turned out to be a symptom of her own insecurities. She later understood that while preoccupied with her quest to discover a new world, her parents were compelled to work long hours to survive. Despite almost a decade in Uruguay, their adopted country remained a difficult cultural and economic environment for them.

Eva capitalized on her freedom to extend her social life by spending nights and weekends with her friends. While still a teen, she yearned for affection and distraction. In her search, she met an unremarkable boy, Gerardo, nicknamed, “Chiquito,” who lived in her building. They saw each other for a while with some frequency. Eva’s first perceived infatuation coincided with her entry into the labor force. There, she met William Melvin who became her first love and husband in 1950, and, within a few years, the father of her daughters.

Chiquito, a neighbor and the son of an older Czech couple, played a transitional role in Eva’s life. She described him as kind and sensitive but with very little ambition in his future. His mother worked as a seamstress, and his father stayed at home which was considered unbecoming for a husband in those days. When Chiquito finished elementary school, he went to work as a mechanic’s apprentice in a local auto repair shop. Through Chiquito, Eva found a useful escort with whom to go for drinks and later partake in gatherings with other couples. In those days it would be unseemly for a woman to be seen drinking at a public establishment without a companion. Eva described those years of youthful infatuation as "joy and rapture." Gradually, however, their interests diverged. As the friendship waned with Chiquito, Eva began quietly seeing William (Bill) Melvin, an American expat businessman living in Uruguay and her senior at Swan, Culbertson, and Fritz. Soon after meeting Bill Eva broke all ties with Chiquito whom she concluded had not been the love of her life after all.

Life in the Switzerland of the South

Dark Days Approach

The 1950's brought significant changes for the Roths. Eva, like most unmarried women of her day, lived under her parent's roof, but as time passed, she became more independent and self-sufficient. Regrettably, just as her salary increased, her family's finances began to spiral downwards. The problems for the Roths began when Walter's employer went bankrupt which resulted in his dismissal. A middle-aged man, Walter could not find employment at a time when Uruguay's economy had slowed. The country's economic hot engine no longer benefitted from the wartime boom.

In his despair, Walter retreated to a dark place. He sought distraction in games of chance. These distractions only served to create greater indebtedness and family conflicts. Disillusioned with his life, Walter began to stray from his marriage. His dalliances gradually became known to Eva and caused her to bear her grief in silence, knowing the pain it would cause her mother. While Walter remained, unemployed Elsie tried to supplement their household income by taking on more English students. The income derived from these classes proved insufficient as debts continued to mount.

Eva continued to thrive in her job and wanted to live in that euphoric moment, but she felt uncomfortable coming home gleefully after work. The air in her home felt tense, filled with acrimony, prompting Eva to search for ways to flee her troubled home whenever possible. On one of those nights, when homelife felt suffocating, she chose to attend a concert at the former Urquiza Theater (rebuilt as the SODRE Auditorium after a fire in 1971). In this theater, Eva often found solace and distraction from her family situations. She frequently attended concerts, an interest her parents cultivated in her from a young age. During the intermission of a performance she attended one Saturday, she ran into her father who introduced her to a woman known to Eva. They interacted cordially but Eva kept the encounter to herself. She knew sharing this chance meeting with her mother would devastate her. Later Eva would learn this interlude had not been an isolated event.

During this dark period in life, Eva consoled herself with her job and business outings with Bill Melvin. At the time, she found Bill a good mentor and charming boss, sociable and astute.

As the Roths continued to accrue debts, they were forced to consider employment outside Montevideo. In 1953, Walter received a position running the tourist concession in Villa Serrana in the state of Minas. The concession known as, El Ventorrillo de la Buena Vista opened in the 1940s and to date is still in operation. It sits on a small sparsely populated, mostly hilly and bucolic region of the country. The Roths lacked the experience necessary to run this concession and found the task and environment unpleasant. Elsie bore the greatest burden needing to staff the kitchen throughout the day. Eva stayed in Montevideo in her parents' apartment while her parents worked in Minas. She would dine with her grandparents, a practice she maintained for many years since their arrival in Uruguay.

She welcomed the peace and stability they provided in their home. She felt comfortable in their home.

After just one year in Minas, the Roths gave up the concession. Walter, ever restless, looked for opportunities in Brazil and finally settled in Paraguay. There, through one of his Czech contacts, he received an offer to work in a knitting factory as merchandiser and sales representative. Eva was devastated. She had considered the possibility of moving to Brazil or Argentina but not an isolated back-water place like Paraguay. Secretly, she had expected to move to the United States where she could further her studies and gain employment. She saw the United States as a country which afforded those with tenacity limitless possibilities. She did not accomplish her goal. Much later in life, she acquired property in the states and visited with great frequency.

For Elsie, the move to Paraguay appeared to be a step back. She hoped Walter would return to Montevideo. She worked harder than ever teaching and doing whatever work she could find to generate income in order to settle Walter's debts. In a last-ditch effort to avoid the move, Elsie sold the last portion of the jewelry she brought from Austria. Despite her industriousness and perseverance, it became necessary to leave Montevideo. Elsie reluctantly joined her husband after struggling for six months.

Elsie moved with mixed emotions to Paraguay in the early part of 1955. Eva would say she moved with "one hand back and one in front." However, G-d had not abandoned them, and his invisible hand manifested itself throughout their time in Paraguay.

Although Eva was just a young child when she left Austria, she recalled in detail, the anguish in her parent's countenance as they sought to leave Austria. She heard their whispers and tried to make sense of the changes that were taking place in her life. She learned to be discrete at an early age as she walked with her parents, cautiously and in fear across places where evil awaited them. In their movements and as they traveled across Europe this young child adapted to changes in language and culture, determined to find a footing. Seeking acceptance in this new environment she remained a friendly and gregarious youngster. This pleasant demeanor allowed her to curry favor with those along her journey, including the crew that brought her and her family to Uruguay.

At 7 years of age, she had already learned how to make herself useful and endeared herself to others. In school she adapted and gained the acceptance of her classmates and elders.

Eva quickly embraced Uruguay as her own. Having an agile mind she easily mastered Spanish as her new language. At home and in her community, she straddled between Austrian and Yiddish balancing two cultures and social norms. Upon entering the workforce, she took up English and worked diligently to become a valuable secretary. She set her goals beyond secretarial work.

Her tenacity and desire for advancement and independence compelled her to work hard and rush to learn the ways of the business world from those around her. She adapted and grew fond of native Uruguayans and with her gregarious nature made friends among her peers and workmates. Even as she flourished, she never took her parents or their sacrifices for granted.

She saw first-hand that even in the darkest moments the steadfast love of her heavenly Father never ceased and His mercies never ended. The disappointment Eva experienced when her parents moved to Uruguay turned out to be an opportunity for Elsie. Putting to use her language skills, Elsie's turned her home into a language academy that provided pride, security and recognition in Paraguay.

In each new circumstance presenting a challenge, Eva sought to persevere and overcome adversity. Over the course of her life, Eva cultivated strong friendships among those in her Jewish community while gaining the trust and respect of the Uruguayans whom she grew to love and appreciate. She warmly embraced humanitarian causes, joining in in philanthropic endeavors which benefitted those in Uruguay and abroad. Witnessing the struggles to form a Jewish state she became a staunch supporter of many philanthropic endeavors benefiting the State of Israel. Moreover, she never forgot the struggles she and her family experienced upon arriving in Uruguay. Eva saw the call to *Tikkun Olam* as extending beyond the Jews in Uruguay and Israel to supporting charitable endeavors and people in need in her homeland of Uruguay.

After entering the workforce Eva learned to navigate a conservative business world in Uruguay which did not openly embrace businesswomen. Yet her charm conquered the naysayers. Before marrying she would travel extensively through Europe and gain a broad view of the world in transition.

While Eva experienced many victories and joys after settling in Uruguay, she also suffered from many insecurities. These too were the side effects of her tumultuous youth. She lived her life fearing the loss of family and friends. Her fear however did not paralyze her. After grieving the loss of her first husband she redirected her attention to her daughters. She used her business acumen to continue to work in private banking and provide aptly for herself and her family's future.

Eva Joins the Workforce

Eva embraced the life she led in Uruguay and chose not to move to Paraguay with her parents due to the broad opportunities available in Montevideo for a young woman of her age. She remained in her parents' apartment while her grandparents resided below in the same apartment in the Old City that had been their home since leaving Europe. Their proximity allowed for some oversight from the grandparents and the joy of their company from time to time. More to Eva's heart, this living arrangement provided greater freedom and an opportunity to explore her womanhood.

At work she forged a deep friendship with Bill Melvin, one of her employers. This much older man became Eva's mentor and companion, and they would frequently socialize after work. Fond of her youthful vitality, he encouraged her to join him on his business functions at the Chamber of Commerce and other trade organization and on special occasions United States Embassy gatherings. She relished those days with him attending business functions. At the time, Bill was still married to a woman named Dorothy, but the two were estranged from one another. Eva's presence as Bill's guest at social functions drew attention for her youth as much as her beauty and elegance.

Bill provided Eva with a window into an altogether different world and culture. Bill came from Canandaigua, New York, a short distance from the city of Rochester. He was born in 1905 into a large Irish Catholic family. One of seven siblings, he spent the formative years of his life in the small town of Canandaigua. He attended school in this then mostly rural part of New York. After finishing high school, he married Dorothy, a local Catholic girl, in a civil ceremony. Bill quickly planned their future on the eve of the Great Depression. No doubt the onset of the depression played a role in his determination to move to South America in 1931 to find his future and fortune. There, he started his career with an American company, Remington

Rand, in their offices in Buenos Aires, Argentina. After a brief time, he moved to Kelox Sales Corporation before making his big move in 1938 to Swan, Culbertson, and Fritz, a multinational finance and investment firm.

The principals of Swan, Culbertson, and Fritz were Americans who began their business enterprise in the Far East. In 1925, Joseph Swan founded the Shanghai investment firm. He was joined by Chester Fritz. Swan had lived in Hong Kong since 1914 working for American Metals, Thereafter the partnership expanded to include C.D. Culbertson, a Texan. Their firm grew rapidly leading them to establish headquarters in New York with subsidiaries in Buenos Aires and then Montevideo. The partnership would hire Bill Melvin, whom they found to be a good fit and a strong prospect, possessing many of the attributes necessary to tackle a changing world order.

Bill an attractive man, excelled as a businessman and quickly became part of the ex-pat community in Buenos Aires. He cultivated an extensive network of business and social contacts as well as relations amongst multinationals and locals. In those days, the American expat community functioned as a closed-knit group. By the early forties, as war enveloped the world, Bill shifted his business role to assist the U.S. Commerce Department and Information Services in 1942. They retained him as an economic analyst with an attractive salary of $3500 a year (equivalent of about $30,000 in 2020). This position placed him within the reach of the U.S. Embassy.

As the war wound down, Bill chose to permanently move to Montevideo, Uruguay. He stayed with the U. S. Embassy as an economic analyst until late 1944 when he returned to his former work with Swan, Culbertson, and Fritz, and his strong ties to the American Chamber of Commerce in Uruguay. His position put him at the intersection of the national and international business communities where he interacted with Uruguayan commerce department representatives and their Department of Commerce counterparts attached to the U.S. Embassy where he remained well-respected and admired.

As Eva continued working with Bill, their friendship grew. As they saw more of each other, he became a frequent visitor to her grandparent's home. He showed great kindness towards her grandparents, neither of whom spoke English and only a modestly mastered Spanish. Bill would spend afternoons with them and, on one special occasion, took them to Punta del Este for the weekend. In those days, Punta del Este was already considered a very attractive beach resort town, a manageable distance from Montevideo. The brief excursion served as a beautiful getaway for this older couple who seldom left Montevideo.

Eva marveled at their friendship and ability to enjoy each other's company through the lengthy outing.

Eva's increasing friendship and warm relations with Bill began to cause tension among the more conservative members of his business circles. As a result, pressure mounted for Bill to reconsider his family status or leave his post. Eva resolved the issue by resigning her position with the company to pursue other employment. Eva did not want to disrupt Bill's well-established career nor place his position in jeopardy. Eva loved her position, the interaction with Bill and the freedom the employment brought her. While working under Bill's guidance she had moved beyond her secretarial tasks and learned much about investments and international finances. Nonetheless, she valued her relationship with Bill more than her job. She knew her skills as secretary were marketable and she would quickly retain other employment.

A Life Changing Trip

Uruguay experienced an economic boom throughout most of the 1940s and extending through the first half of the 1950s. The growth mostly from exports of beef and wool products. Uruguay escaped much of the privation of the war years. It had no first-hand experience with the recovery from the war which so many others endured for more than a decade. The harsh recovery fell to those that allied themselves to the wrong side as much as those who were caught up in the war.

Eva, no longer a child, yearned for romance and adventure in her life. Needing to distance herself from Bill and anxious for a change of scenery, Eva reached out to her close friend, Ruth. The two energetic young women gathered their resources and began to map out an extended trip to Europe. Eva and Ruth had much in common. Both came to be in Uruguay after their families escaped the war in Europe, but Ruth's family came from Berlin, Germany, and Eva's from neighboring Austria. Together, they planned a trip seeking to discover parts of the world outside Uruguay. At the same time, they sought to explore their families' history and perhaps learn the whereabouts their surviving relatives.

The two set out in 1953. Both were just twenty, full of curiosity about how life and the world would shape them. They both needed closure about the fate of their relatives trapped in Europe during the war. In that pivotal year, Eva and Ruth boarded an Italian ship heading north from Montevideo. The ship made stops in Porto Alegre, Rio de Janeiro, and Santos in Brazil, all port cities unfamiliar to them. Near the port of Recife, the ship veered east for the 2,500 nautical mile Atlantic crossing. After leaving the coast of South America, the ship sailed slowly towards the African coast. After almost two weeks, it made port in Dakar, the largest city in Senegal, then a part of French

West Africa, a French colony. This extended stop put them in a sweat drenched, arid land filled by a mélange of color and foreign languages. Dakar had been a Portuguese settlement serving as the base for the Atlantic slave trade which later became a French colony for the French colonial empire in the early 20th century. In the 1950s, Dakar, had rebounded from its role in the world war and served as a major port and commerce center for the French and West Africa. It boasted French styled night clubs and restaurants frequented by mostly French survivors freed from internment camps after the war. Dakar would provide their first glimpse of what they would experience along their travels.

After leaving Dakar, the ship sailed north on the Atlantic, crossing the Strait of Gibraltar into the Mediterranean and into the Ligurian Sea before docking in their last port, Genoa, Italy. Eva and Ruth debarked with their array of suitcases to spend a month traveling throughout Italy. Their course took them south to Rome with a visit to Vatican City. From there, they headed further south to Naples and the Amalfi Coast where they stayed in small hotels and met up with two friends they knew from Uruguay. These friends were sailors who were well acquainted with the area took the two of them sightseeing and enjoying the life around the south of Italy. The four enjoyed their time together as Eva and Ruth experienced the natural beauty and history of this area. From Naples, they headed back north and determined to split up in Venice or perhaps Milan. Ruth could not obtain a visa into Germany as it remained under Soviet control. Moreover, she had no desire to return to Germany and instead chose to travel to Switzerland by herself.

Eva, now on her own, headed for Vienna. Elsie, Walter, and perhaps family acquaintances provided a few contacts to whom Eva could avail herself in seeking details about her diasporic European family. Upon arriving in Vienna, Eva met up with a gentleman who took her to her grandfather's former textile business location. The visit may have given her some insights into the textiles it produced, but not much about her family or where they had gone after the war.

Although Martin and Frieda, Eva's paternal grandparents, found their way to Uruguay after the start of the war, Elsie's parents just vanished. Eva may have tried to reach out to family and friends, as this could have been the last chance she had to see them or perhaps correspond with them if Oskar and Giselle survived in Austria or elsewhere in Europe in search of safe haven.

Eva did not gain much information from the labyrinth of bureaucracies in Vienna. At the time, Austria was not transparent about its role in the destruction of Jewish communities in their country. The same was true of Germany which then struggled with the Cold War, facing squabbles between east and west and the departure of British occupation in favor of civilian rule. Eva did not obtain confirmation on the fate of her grandparents and other relatives until sometime later when she received International Red Cross records which documented Oskar and Gisela Zwieback's names as among those having perished in a camp in Yugoslavia. Records maintained (index cards of those deported from Vienna which were held by the Israelitische Kultusgemeinde in Vienna) by the United States Holocaust Memorial Museum show that both Oskar and Gisela Zwieback were deported to a camp along the Sava River in Yugoslavia (now part of Croatia), believed to be Jasenovac. Jasenovac unlike most camps was run by the Ustaše, a fascist regime allied with the Nazi state. The sparse records from this camp indicate the Zwiebacks did not survive. Likewise, Ruth and her family learned the destiny of their relatives through the Red Cross. Sometime after the war, Ruth learned that her grandparents had perished in a camp in Riga, Latvia.

After a bitter-sweet stay in Vienna, Eva reconnected with Ruth in London. There, Eva stayed with Elsie's relatives, most likely her mother's cousin, Gretel, who had left Prague for England in the late 1930s. London, still recovering from the bombings by the Germans during the Blitz was a city in transition. Some areas were in reconstruction while others showed deep scars from the war. For Eva and Ruth, London provided a time of respite from the disappointing efforts in their mission to learn the whereabouts of their respective European families. After a short rest in London, they headed south by train to Poole to cross the English Channel by ferry into the port of Cherbourg in France where the now inseparable friends took a bus into Paris to discover the "city of lights".

Paris provided an opulent and more joyful climax to their trip. Paris, which remained occupied by the Nazis throughout most of the war did not experience massive destruction from aerial bombing. While in Paris, Ruth and Eva had opportunity to visit the Eiffel Tower, museums that reopened after the war, grand houses of worship, and most memorable, an evening at the Paris Opera House. Eva had cultivated a passion for classical music from an early age. The trip to the Paris Opera House was the realization of a fairytale evening. In the traditions of the day, a visit to the opera required long, fashionable gowns and provided an elegant and grandiose environment unlike any she had experienced in her lifetime. Before departing Paris, they headed out to the Hippodrome de Vincennes, where each made a small wager of 50 Francs.

The Paris trip, however, came with its share of mishaps. While in Paris, Eva lost her wallet. Concerned over hotel security both women carried all their travel money in their wallets. There were no room safes in their lodgings, and the main safe would be controlled by the prying eyes of hotel employees. When Eva failed to find her wallet, she had no choice but to phone home for a lifeline. Bill came through in spades. Not only did he wire funds to Eva, but he also booked for them a week in one of the most elegant hotels in Paris.

After finishing their unforgettable trip to Paris, they headed south to Nice where another of Elsie's relatives, a hospitable cousin, provided lodging, home cooked meals, and promenades through the city. Life in Nice, the heart of the French Riviera, greatly differed from the elegance and formalities of Paris. The pace slowed down considerably as the seaside town displayed a more congenial environment. Their touring took on a more familial nature as the young couple and their children made them feel welcome.

From France, they travelled by train to Spain and Portugal on the final leg of their extensive and life-affirming

European trip. Post-war Spain remained under the grip of rightist strongman, Generalissimo Francisco Franco. His Guardia Civil kept a powerful hold on the country which made travel through Spain potentially dangerous. Neither Eva nor Ruth can quite remember whether it was in Cadiz or Malaga where they crossed the strait of Gibraltar to reach Tangiers in Morocco. Once in Tangiers, they had their first encounter with a Muslim city and an Arab *souk* (open-air bazaar). From Morocco, they crossed back over to Portugal for their return to South America on the lavish and once revered Pan American Airways.

The flight from Lisbon took them to Rio de Janeiro where they spent a few days of warmth on the beaches before settling into the tranquil life of Montevideo. The trip had exceeded the planned month of touring, and in those months away from home, Eva discovered her passion for travel and embraced her fearless and adventurous nature. After their trip, both returned to their homes in Uruguay with a greater confidence and much enhanced worldview. Despite Eva's failure to learn the fates of her family members, she described her trip as "a great emotional and educational adventure." In the brief period of her travels, Eva encountered a new world and made new friends, some with whom she established bonds that endured through correspondence for many years. After this experience, she would continue to travel frequently to distant lands across the world while she remained physically able to do so. During her time married to Bill, Eva would travel to Europe every other year. With Herbert her travels took her to the Greek Isles, Australia and often to Israel, where Herbert had family and business relations.

The first European trip also represented yet another tipping point in Eva's life. While the touring brought lighthearted and enjoyable moments, the trip also provided a great sense of accomplishment. The travels for both Eva and Ruth led to a profound understanding of a world in recovery. Throughout their stops, they witnessed the enormous devastation brought on by the war. They left Uruguay as young naïve girls knowing few details of the war's impact upon London and the European continent, and many aspects of the war they knew only from shared stories and by reading limited accounts in their local paper of the events that took place. Eva and Ruth were both young as the war festered and could not appreciate the magnitude of what transpired on a macro level. With pain and incredulity, they learned that, despite following the impact of the war on their relatives and friends, they could not imagine its vast effects across all countries and segments of society.

Throughout Europe they found that, eight years after the war ended, most cities remained in ruins. Caserta, near Naples, provided the most searing images for them. Nothing seemed to be left standing, and people were still living in half bombed- out basements or shelters in hollowed out tree trunks. As they moved about from place to place, they were deeply touched by the immense poverty and lack of basic nutrition. Orchards and farms remained bare causing shortages of fruits and vegetables throughout the region.

In London, they found that few living there had moved past the hardships of the war. The conversations among the British population remained about the devastation and loss of life. The populace in London shared painful memories of the *blitz* that devastated their magnificent and densely populated metropolis. In Spain, the conversations amongst Spaniards were mostly about the Civil War that had ravaged them from 1936 to 1939. Those conversations were most discrete as strongman Generalisimo Francisco Franco kept a tight grip on dissention.

Eva and Ruth returned to Montevideo committed to their enduring and deep friendship. Their experience forced them to look in the mirror and put away their childish ways. They now shared a painful understanding of a world where good and evil had clashed and assessed the prize paid for good to triumph over evil. They learned much about each other and never had occasion to quarrel. As a result, in later years, both would return to Europe frequently, not so much in search of adventure, but to experience a different dimension of their lives and reconnect with family and their descendants throughout the world. Eva would now turn her attention towards marriage and establishing a family.

The New Mrs. Melvin

Eva needed to determine where she stood in her relationship with Bill. By the time she returned home, Dorothy had left Bill and moved back to the United States. In 1954, the process of divorce, even state-side, moved slowly and with difficulty. As the separation ensued, Bill and Eva continued to see each other more openly. Eva was anxious to leave the horrors of Europe behind and deepen her relationship with Bill. They concluded the year spending their summer in a little cottage they rented in Punta del Este and took pleasure in the resort town. Elsie, aware that Eva had been seeing Bill, longed that they would have the opportunity to marry.

In that pivotal year, Eva also started new employment with the auditing firm of H. Martin and Co. where she enjoyed pleasant working conditions as the firm's sole secretary.

Bill's divorce was finalized in Argentina, but the two could not marry there or in Uruguay due to laws in place which made remarriage impossible. At the time, the ordinances in predominantly Catholic countries did not recognize the dissolution of a binding marriage through divorce. As a result, in January of 1956, Bill and Eva were married in a civil ceremony in the town of San Lorenzo in the outskirts of Asuncion, Paraguay. Afterwards they celebrated their nuptials in the home of Eva's joyful parents before returning to Uruguay. Once in Uruguay they headed to Punta del Este to celebrate their wedding and new life with their friends at the golf club. Eva was finally Mrs. Melvin. She had waited a long time for this day, and her tenacity had paid off.

After their wedding, Bill and Eva took an extended honeymoon trip enjoying time in the snow resort in Bariloche. They stayed away almost three months traveling throughout the United States. The last stop on their trip was Rochester, New York, Bill's hometown, and where his family resided. Eva met his extended family here, including Bill's 3 surviving brothers and sisters. Initially, the visit posed a challenge for Eva. Bill had left home 25 years earlier and now returned with a Jewish wife, 28 years his younger. Eva guardedly concealed her feared rejection; however, she swiftly found Bill's family to be warm, jovial, and informal in their lifestyle. The family welcomed her like one of their own. The New Yorkers forged strong family ties with the laidback Uruguayans which remain to this day. Many of Bill's descendants, now great-aunts and cousins, continue to reside in the Western New York and maintain strong friendships with Bill and Eva's children and grandchildren.

William Melvin

Eva Roth Melvin entertaining

Upon the newlyweds' return to Montevideo, they resumed their social life among Bill's business circles and Eva's Jewish friends. Among the Jewish circles, Bill acquired the affectionate nickname "Melvinski," a true mensch to all. Eva relished her new status and the acceptance it brought. They started their lives in what Eva described as "true happiness." As a young newlywed, she elegantly decorated their apartment to her taste without going overboard. As a result of Bill's position, they were now entertaining businessmen and hobnobbing with U. S. Chamber of Commerce personnel and at times staffers from United States Embassy. Bill and Eva attended parties and social gatherings at the U.S. Embassy where Eva perceived herself as the young princess. Like all marriages, this one had some difficulties to overcome. Bill's job required attendance at business meetings and commitments, which limited their time for pleasurable pursuits. As a young bride Eva wanted Bill to spend time with her, which was not always possible. Bill worked long hours and at times came home stressed. Once home the two imbibed liberally which at times lead to squabbles. Despite age and cultural differences, Bill showed great love and affection towards his new wife, lavishing her with many gifts.

After settling into married life, Eva began volunteer work at the Women International Zionist Organization, the WIZO. WIZO was akin to Hadassah, a worldwide Jewish women's charitable organization. The ladies of this organization were younger, most of whom were in her age group. Over the years, she established lasting friendships and ties with a number of these women. Finding her place within the organization, she formally joined the WIZO and remained an active member most of her adult life. She found room for camaraderie, a warm and candid exchange of family life, and events of all dimensions. The friends from the WIZO comprised a large part of the fabric of her social interactions as they engaged in all types of activities together, whether charitable or simply pleasurable. Eva showed a generous heart towards the poor and those struggling in both Uruguay and the State of

Israel. Throughout her life, she remained committed to charitable endeavors and shared her bounty generously.

On January 10th, 1957, Eva gave birth to their first daughter, Brenda Ann. She felt joyful upon the birth of her first born and described her as a beautiful, red-headed baby. Bill, now 51, rejoiced at the birth of his first child. He considered Brenda special among his "loves." The three Melvins were a happy bunch, and just as they settled into married and family life, Eva learned she was pregnant with her second daughter. She met this news with a brief bout of melancholy out of fear of what this pregnancy might portend as Brenda's pregnancy resulted in a lengthy and difficult delivery.

The birth of Deborah Louise on February 6th, 1959, filled Eva with overwhelming love for her second child. Converse to Brenda's birth, Eva would gloat that Debbie's delivery came blessedly "pain free, marvelous, and quick." Eva proudly paraded the halls of the maternity ward a few hours after the delivery, bragging to her friends of the ease by which she had delivered her second child even though Bill did not reach the hospital in time to witness Debbie's delivery. Debbie's birth coincided with the start of the Lenten season's carnival week, and Bill was away at a beach resort in Solis with friends and colleagues. He came a day later after preparing himself emotionally to greet the newborn and his wife. Despite Eva's momentary anxiety over Bill's delay, she remained joyful over her second daughter and her ease in the delivery. Prior to the birth of the girls, Bill and Eva had agreed that if she were to give birth to boys, they would be circumcised, but the issue never arose as they had no other children. The family was now complete.

A few months after Debbie's birth, Bill and Eva moved to a larger home in Montevideo, and Eva once again took care to use her gifts to tastefully decorate the home to her liking. Both Eva and Bill embraced a new home life which now included children and blended friendships. Harry Gordon, known as, "El Ingles" (the Englishman) and Bill's best friend, turned out to be married to Irene Rosenburg, one of the passengers on the *MS Copacabana*. Upon reconnecting, Eva struck a lifelong friendship with Irene. She remained a close friend with whom Eva could confide and relate when the men were engaged in more serious discussions.

As Eva transitioned to her role as the mother of two young girls, her mom and dad remained in Paraguay. Eva yearned to be closer to her mother, but Elsie was making a life with her language school in Paraguay and could not spend much time in Uruguay. Eva clung to her grandparents, Martin and Frieda who continued to live in the old city, in the place they occupied prior to Elsie's move to Paraguay. They remained her closest ancestral ties; all other relatives having passed or made a life elsewhere as an outgrowth of the Jewish diaspora.

Shortly after Debbie's birth, Elsie and Walter invited Eva's grandparents to fly to Asunción, Paraguay, such that they could see for themselves how life had markedly improved for Eva's mother and father in Asunción. Elsie had already established The Language Institute of Miss Elsie Roth, and they were basking in a time of economic comfort. The school operated out of their residence in a set-aside area which boasted 8 classrooms with classes scheduled between 8 AM and 10 PM for 6 days a week. The school facility included a dining room for lunch inspired by Elsie's European recipes and rooms to accommodate an afternoon siesta. Elsie who spoke English flawlessly, operated the only English academy in Asuncion, and many government officials passed through Miss Elsie Roth's School of Languages.

As Debbie and Brenda grew older, they would spend their winter vacations (July) with their grandparents in Asuncion where they would fly on Pluna or LAP (then the Uruguayan national airlines) for a two-hour flight to their grandparent's home. A highlight of their time with their grandmother came when both Debbie and Brenda were allowed to sit-in on school's English classes where they could interact with other teachers and students. Elsie always made time from the language school's schedule to spend time with her granddaughters. For Debbie and Brenda, the trips to Paraguay were also an opportunity to see their grandmother's involvement in Jewish philanthropy and interactions with her social circles where they were both treated warmly. In Paraguay, both girls learned to communicate with Elsie's domestics who only spoke in *Guarani*, the indigenous language in Paraguay. For Elsie, the school, which she ran by herself, provided fulfilment and steady income. Walter, however remained restless and could not find employment to his liking. He remained unemployed the rest of his life. Since Walter had no part in the school, he felt isolated, neglected. This led to other pursuits which led to distrust in the marriage and squabbles with Elsie.

Martin's first trip to Asuncion to celebrate his 90th birthday with his family was also his first airplane ride. *Opi* and *Oma*, as Eva affectionately called her grandparents remained in Paraguay for a month. During their stay, they toured and visited the more attractive parts of the Asuncion. The rest of their days were spent with Elsie at the school assessing with glee what she had built-up since leaving Uruguay. They also spent some time with Walter, their son and met a several of their family acquaintances in social gatherings Elsie organized.

After experiencing life in Paraguay with their family, Martin and Frieda left the very warm climes of Asuncion, to return to Montevideo as a bitterly cold winter set in. The change in climates may not have agreed with *Opi* who took ill upon his return home. He remained bedridden for two months under his wife's care. Scarcely three months after his 90th birthday Martin passed away as peacefully and dignified as he had lived. Eva recalls visiting him twice a day during the months he suffered from his illness. Sadly, the day he died, Eva and the family were on their way back from Buenos Aires. They were called and asked to meet Elsie and Walter at Carrasco Airport which signaled to Eva what she knew would be heartbreaking news. While Eva anticipated that *Opi's* days were few, her understanding did not diminish the deep grief she experienced upon his passing.

After the funeral, Eva's parents returned to Asunción. *Omi* remained while Eva determined where it would be best for the grandmother she loved so dearly to live out her life. At the time, *Omi* was severely afflicted with Alzheimer and could not live independently, and, after a few tests, the family determined it would be best for her to live in Asunción. *Omi* strenuously opposed the move. Ultimately, Eva moved her to the "Comunidad Israelita," (Jewish home for the aged) where she received good care and continued to live until her death. Eva and her daughters visited frequently throughout the eight years she remained in the care facility.

Eva loved and stayed close to her grandmother throughout her life, but as *Omi* grew feeble, Eva embraced the burdensome responsibility of her ongoing care. *Omi* represented Eva's only surviving relative in Uruguay and over time she found it difficult to spend long hours in the home for the aged, feeling suffocated by the surroundings of its fragile elderly residents. Despite the oppressive and somber environment, Eva believed that she had done her best to keep her grandmother content.

As this chapter in Eva's life ended with Frieda's death, she refocused her attention to her daughters and husband. Her days of caring and mourning her grandmother, had caused Eva great sadness. With each loss, she felt pulled from the memories she dearly embraced. She needed to snap out of the tormenting sadness by spending time and pouring out her love on Brenda and Debbie. They became her pride and fulfillment, and her relations with Bill also strengthened in the years following the death of her grandparents. Although her parents remained in Paraguay, she remained close to them as well. They visited frequently, when school was not in session. Eva, the ever-prolific letter writer, never lost touch with them. As Brenda and Debbie grew older, they spent many seasonal vacations with their grandparents in Paraguay. Planning and arranging these vacations for her girls brought peace of mind to Eva and Bill who travelled extensively to Europe and the United States.

Deborah and Brenda in their pre-school uniforms

Debbie with her father, Bill in Rochester, NY

Summers in Bileva

Montevideo has a few local beaches, and there are several resorts east of the capital. One beach resort, however, stands out for Uruguayans and international tourists alike: Punta del Este. Seated at the geographic point which separates the Atlantic Ocean from the River Plate, this resort became a destination for the very affluent and influential political elite and financial magnates in the early 1960s. Most seasonal tourists came from the metropolitan area of Buenos Aires, just a short flight away. By the sixties, the resort of Punta del Este, its restaurants, and nighttime venues were well developed. Although the resort within the department of Maldonado had a census of 15,000 permanent residents, it's population could swell to hundreds of thousand visitors between December and February each year.

In this pivotal decade, Punta also became center stage to global and hemispheric economists as well as those engaged in the Southern cone regional development community. Punta made its mark on the political world stage when dignitaries came together there to sign the Charter for the Alliance for Progress at a summit in the winter of 1961. Later as a decade of political turmoil raced across Latin America, Punta del Este drew finance ministers and members of the Inter-American bank to its wind beaten beaches. While leaders met in the tranquility of the resort, the capital sizzled with a growing movement of leftist guerrilla fighters known as the Tupamaros. By the end of the decade, these urban leftist fighters had caused massive upheaval. Their actions lead to the declaration of a state of siege in Latin America's bastion of democracy. Although Uruguay escaped the era of massive destabilization that impacted neighboring countries, its economy and social fiber were deeply shaken.

It is in this place, Punta del Este, where Eva and Bill chose to create their own oasis in a home, they called "BIL-EVA." In 1956, Bill and Eva began construction of this house in the resort town. The project started as a modest endeavor in which to spend weekends in the summer. The plans called for a 300 square meter structure near the water's edge, but, as time passed, the plans grew more expansive and included gardens of 2100 square meters. The quaint cottage soon became a palatial setting. Once completed, BILEVA drew the attention and admiration of onlookers and acquaintances. Eva took pride in this summer enclave, and it provided an ideal distraction from the brewing tensions in the Capital in the 1960s and early 1970s.

BILEVA became the vacation destination for the Melvins for almost 17 years. The times spent in the home and in the resort were jolly with many social gatherings. Despite brisk activity, it also provided solace and time for relaxation. BILEVA became a place to refresh, but also to escape and engage in the fantasy that all was well in the Switzerland of South America. When Brenda and Debbie were young, Eva and the girls would leave for Punta in December and stay throughout the summer, not returning to the capital until the latest possible date in March. This resort home provided a place where the girls could enjoy their carefree youth. Bill worked in the Capital and joined them on weekends and extended weeks when work allowed it since he too sought time in their sanctuary.

As the girls grew into their teen years, they had many opportunities to attend parties and gatherings among regular vacationers, and, for Bill and Eva, these summer days were times of dinner parties with friends. These included close friends like the Gordons, ex-pats, diplomats, and their families. The dinners would often extend to 50 or 60 people gathered on their lawn. In this place, life revolved around opulent social gatherings. Adults pridefully donned their most exclusive designer labels, ensembles, and jewelry as drinks flowed liberally, and no one lacked. Youths trailed at a distance while their nannies and caretakers kept watch. Eva recalls one particularly hot summer, when they hosted a party attended by the U.S. Ambassador to Uruguay. He came with an entourage and security detail to take part in a party they dubbed "Pisco and Seafood." This was one of many such gatherings that drew the social elite as well as those vying to be in their company.

Life in Punta del Este, revolved around beach outings, sports, extravagance in dining and celebration of family traditions. For the Melvins, Christmas Eve was always very special in their home. On this festive day, the family would trim a large Christmas tree, a tradition observed in the United States by the secular and religious alike. At midnight on Christmas Eve, adults and children would gather to receive much anticipated gifts. In the Melvin tradition, Eva received her most lavish gift of the year from Bill on this evening. One year, Bill surprised Eva with a generous gift of Israeli bonds which made Eva laugh a bit as this was traditionally a Christian day of celebration. This gift served to accentuate Bill's deep affection for Eva knowing her passion for the State of Israel. This gift turned into a very wise investment as the Uruguayan economy plunged into a downward spiral. Eva and Bill usually hosted two very dear older couples on Christmas Eve as they had no family of their own with whom to celebrate. They would dine with the Melvins and then enjoy being part of the "shower" of gifts. This became a practice adopted by Debbie and her family once in the United States.

For Eva Christmas and other holidays celebrated in her home brought delightful opportunities to display her creativity and elegance. She loved all aspects of planning and organizing such events, bringing together family and friends. Most of these events included music, dancing and lavish food displays. These events were always antidotes to Eva's darker days.

PARADISE LOST

THE END OF AN ERA

The small peaceful nation of Uruguay distinguished itself from most of its hemispheric neighbors by boasting relatively stable economies with democratically elected leaders. Uruguayans enjoyed one of the more educated and culturally advanced societies in the continent. This all seemed in jeopardy as the leftist leaning Tupamaros, set out to wreak havoc. These malcontents were bent on disrupting the establishment through a series of high-profile kidnappings and bank robberies. Their objective was to focus on the economic inequities between the wealthy and what they perceived as the impoverished working class.

The disruption in the economy resulted in fear and discord within political factions.

In 1965 at the invitation of the Uruguayan government, the United States Office of Public Safety, part of the USAID sent trainers and advisors to Uruguay. These were tasked with staving off insurgents and providing a disciplined approach for the country's security apparatus. As the government's attempts to control evolving violence and chaos failed in 1968, Uruguay's President Jorge Pacheco Areco issued a "state of siege". This measure, however, failed to restore stability. Violence continued, political prisoners in Punta Carretas Penitentiary swelled to unsustainable levels, and the unrest culminated with the kidnapping and murder of U. S. OPS, Chief Public Service Adviser, Dan Mitrione, on August 10, 1970. These dark moments in Uruguay's history would be shared with the world in a quasi-fictional French/Italian movie aptly titled "*State of Siege*."

Back at BILEVA, grand celebrations continued as the Melvin's welcomed a new decade, their future remaining bright despite the deteriorating security of their country. That year, Eva and Bill invited Eva's parents to come from Montevideo to share in the Christmas Day festivities. Christmas Day coincided with the celebration of the Roth's 40th wedding anniversary, and, a month later, Bill and Eva would be celebrating their 15th year of a fulfilling marriage blessed with two beautiful daughters. In theatrical fantasy, they also planned the celebrations that would take place in another ten years. They would toast to Elsie and Walter's golden wedding anniversary, as well as the Melvins' silver anniversary. Eva believed that BILEVA signified a sort of "liberation," although she could not articulate how such a feeling came about, but perhaps it could have stemmed from a feeling of having a brief escape from the uncertainty that engulfed her country.

Eva had everything she wanted or needed, and Bill gave her much latitude to do as she pleased throughout the year. Punta, however, allowed her freedom to move about carefree among her circle of friends without the threat of gossips likely to be at work in the more socially formal living rooms of the capital. In Punta, she enjoyed creating her "garden" by cultivating friends and making memories that would carry her throughout the years.

For Eva, BILEVA became her cherished summer home until its sale in 1973. As turmoil swept through Uruguay, Bill and Eva considered emigrating to Spain. Eva opposed such plans because she thought that in such a far-off place, she would end up a lonely "widow." She saw no benefit in having to adjust to a new culture and social environment, only hardships and difficulties. Thankfully for Eva, these plans never materialized.

Thinking back, BILEVA provided years of joyful memories, with the occasional discourse that arise in any marriage. One could always look forward to guests, parties, family reunions, and all kinds of fun at BILEVA. This home held treasured memories of Eva's time with Debbie and Brenda growing up into loving and caring young women. For Eva, the day they sold the house was one of mourning. Years after they sold the house, Eva would drive by the house with great longing, remembering the memories made there with her family and friends. She sometimes contemplated the thought that, if the opportunity arose, she would buy back the house. While Eva owned other homes in Punta del Este throughout the remainder of her life, none compared in the joyful memories BILEVA evoked.

Bill and Eva's life in their Uruguayan homeland provided an extensive array of friends, relations, and a host of social diversions. In the winter months, they traveled outside the capital for weekend jaunts. Sometimes, close friends accompanied them. Through these and other events, Eva's marriage to Bill grew in love and understanding.

While married to Bill, Eva may have engaged in a fleeting interlude, which she described as insignificant. Eva recalls a friendship to a distinguished American official stationed in southeast Asia. He was married and the father of two. He spent little time in Uruguay as his post kept him abroad. While overseas, he corresponded with Eva and shared unspeakable details of the horrors of that war. Nothing came of Eva's admiration for this American; rather, she bore great respect for his intellect and recalled him with fondness. Eva would see him again in 1982, now aged and despondent but glad for their friendship. He and Bill had worked together and enjoyed a close friendship.

One Christmas, before they sold BILEVA, Bill gave Eva a trip to Europe which Eva would take by herself. She postponed it for some time waiting for Brenda to return from an unpleasant six-month scholarship stay with a host family in the state of Arizona in the United States. Brenda's stay in the states was planned as an enriching experience, but the host family turned out to live in a household filled with conflict. The home environment looked to be culturally and socially incompatible with Brenda's upbringing. The host family expected Brenda to be a caretaker to their children rather than a guest in their home which led to great distress for Brenda. Once she returned, however, Eva proceeded to organize her trip to Europe in July of 1973.

Eva planned an expansive trip to escape her utter state of *ennui*. This trip had no particular purpose or goals, only a desire to get away. Although Eva knew of Bill's malignant cancer of the larynx since Bill had been quietly undergoing radiation treatments Bill insisted, she not postpone or cancel the trip. Two days before departing, Eva received a call from Bill's doctor who confronted Eva with the seriousness of Bill's illness. Shockingly, the doctor also urged Eva to go on her trip. In this way, Bill would not suspect the grave state of his health. In hindsight and upon reflection, Eva questioned how she proceeded with her trip and what drew her to do so.

Brenda and Debbie took on the task of caring for their dad while Eva travelled. Eva found that Bill recovered during her absence! In this inexplicable miracle, she found him much thinner and changed, but invigorated, nonetheless. Although Eva did not expected Bill to recover from his cancer based on the dire prognosis his doctor had described, this illness became the beginning of a steep decline for Bill. Despite his initial recovery, Eva continued to experience a sense of severe melancholy and depression.

The remaining years of Bill's life were difficult for Eva. In the years following his initial illness, Bill became combative and difficult. He desired to retire from his employment and move to Spain after growing disenchanted with the Uruguay he had loved. Bill's perception of Uruguay had changed. The country he believed, no longer appeared secure or welcoming to Americans. As a result, Bill and Eva took a lengthy trip through Spain in 1973. They returned the following year with the girls, but, while in Spain, they selected schools for Debbie and Brenda and chose the place where they were determined to establish their new residence, upon leaving Uruguay.

Delays followed, and Eva became weary and emotionally drained as she witnessed Bill's decline. These years were bitter and draining on Eva's soul. Bill's heart began to give out, and he lost the strength necessary to undertake the monumental move to Europe. Added to these obstacles were Eva and Bill's attachment to the material things of this world. They loved their home near the tip of Teru Street in Montevideo. The two had built this home over the course of two and a half years, and it became a source of pride and satisfaction. Eva would remain there after Bill's passing and well into the 1980s. During these dark days, Bill could only watch as Eva became downcast.

In times of sorrow, Eva looked to her daughters for comfort and drew towards Brenda, her eldest. While close to Debbie, she felt challenged by her strength of character, and they often butted heads. Debbie gravitated towards her father during this season. Yet, over the years and after

Bill's death, the family dynamics changed; Debbie and Eva grew to be the best of friends. Debbie supported Eva, and Eva confided to her the great anguish she felt after Bill's death. Debbie, then young, vulnerable, and dealing with her own grief, endeavored to counsel and support her mom. After a time of mourning, Eva struggled to begin a new life, deal with her loneliness, and justify her desire for a new relationship with her friend from youth, Herbert Donner.

Elsie remained Eva's true north during these years. Throughout Bill's illness, she would frequently travel from Asuncion on weekends just to support and encourage Eva to revive her spirits. Bill occasionally urged Elsie to come to Uruguay because he could not cope with Eva's state of mind. As a caring mother, Elsie would travel on Bill's urging counseling Eva to undertake nurturing activities which might overcome her despondency. She understood Eva's situation having lived through so many challenges in her youth and sorrow in her married life. After Bill's death Elsie and other close friends living in Montevideo stepped in and drew close to Eva to provide her with a much-needed safety-net.

"We are but a mist that appears for a little bit and then vanishes." The Letter of James 4:14

After the sale of BILEVA and easing back into the chaos engulfing the country, Eva became intensely aware of the decline and aging of many of those closest to her. She had married Bill when they were both vivacious and energetic, despite the 28-year difference in their ages. Those differences became acutely evident with Bill's downturn. As Eva grappled with Bill's deterioration, she could not ignore similar circumstances in her parents who were Bill's contemporaries.

Bill's last months were profoundly painful to Eva and their teenage daughters. As Eva realized that her beloved's life was at an end, she felt overwhelmed with grief. She increasingly drew inward and behaved harshly towards those around her. Others perceived her as insensitive and uncaring for her husband's pain and poor health, but Eva would argue it was quite the opposite. She treasured the conversations with him in those days when both knew Bill's death was imminent, she recorded many of their conversations and cherished them often after he left her.

Eva lost Bill in 1976.

The family mourned him deeply as did his colleagues and friends. Bill's death was soon followed by Elsie in 1978 and then her father, Walter in 1980. Those years of deep sorrow were filled with doubts and insecurities as a vast segment of Eva's emotional support system collapsed. She felt that those whom she needed and loved abandoned her. Although the losses were all brought about by aging and illness, the absence of loved ones brought on fear and anxiety for her. In this season, Eva struggled to put dark thoughts behind. Her mind, however, remained consumed with the apprehension of further illnesses and tragedies. Eva exposed her frailty, sharing her worries with her close confidants about how she would face the world on her own and remain strong. She pondered her ability to provide for Debbie and Brenda's education and where and from whom she would derive guidance. In this time of great insecurity, she longed for another man to fill her life and void.

Eva Regains her Footing

Finding Light in Darkness

Upon Bill's death, issues arose concerning his business interest at Swan, Culbertson, and Fritz. Eva had been out of the work force for some time and did not feel psychologically equipped to grapple with business responsibilities, yet Bill's business partners came from Europe and encouraged her to carry on with the enterprise anyway. Despite Eva's mental paralysis, after Bill's death, Elsie and other close friends nudged her to persevere. In hindsight, the business became Eva's source of hope and provided a much-needed sense of purpose. It allowed her to find a firm footing in her life and undertake meaningful work.

Eva's transition was aided by the support she received from Leonor, her trusted administrator and confidant. For Eva, the idea of making money and being able to spend it without having to give an account appealed to her. This is not to say that Eva and Bill quarreled over her spending, but for Eva, deriving an income was more about feeling fulfilled and relevant. Income also provided the means to continue her generous philanthropy.

"Sorrow and mourning may come, but joy comes in the morning." ***Psalms* 30:5**

Now a young widow in her late 40s, Eva contemplated her next steps. She found herself "free" and unentangled, something she had once considered to be a desirable position.

Sadly, being alone and "free" did not provide a pleasant environment for Eva. She needed someone for whom to care and provide. She desperately needed to feel wanted and loved. The girls were now grown-up, finding their own paths with boyfriends and marriage in their sights. She hoped for a miracle that would show her a way forward. In time, G-d provided one. In the months after Bill's death, Eva looked for opportunities to fill her days, particularly when finding herself in the silence of her empty home and late into the night when she needed warmth and companionship. To fill her evenings, she chose to take up art classes and participate in other activities. Two months after Bill passed away; while attending an Art History class, she ran into Herbert Donner. Eva had not seen him in several years although both were part of Montevideo's tightly knit Jewish community. Eva knew that his wife, Paloma, had passed away only a month after what Eva described as Bill's hard death.

After a few passing conversations, Herbert and Eva rekindled their friendship from youth. They spoke while in class and thereafter agreed to dine together. Eva and Herbert spent hours talking about each other's respective children and former spouses who had departed this life. As they shared stories, they were captivated by all that transpired in their lives since the days when they were in the Hebraica Macabi together 27 years back. Although they had led different lives for a quarter of a century, they had many common friends drawn from the Jewish community of Montevideo.

Eva felt a bond and connection with Herbert as they were of similar backgrounds, and education. Both were born in Vienna and had left Austria with their parents at a young age to escape the Nazi onslaught. Herbert was four years older than Eva when he and his family arrived in Uruguay, and his family left Austria by train to Genoa, Italy and then by cruise liner to Montevideo. Their respective families having fled Austria after the *Anschluss*.

The Donners tried, but failed, to obtain a visa to the United States because Austrians desiring to emigrate to the United States faced a ten-year waiting period under its quota system. Knowing the risks of staying in Europe they opted to purchase visas of dubious provenance to Uruguay, and they used these to obtain first class round-trip from Austria to Uruguay. The family traveled as tourists and walked a tight rope similarly to Eva's family. Providentially, the Donners, who owned a shirt company in Vienna, purchased their visas to travel to Uruguay on December **12**, 1938. They knew the visas were suspect, but, having little recourse, took their chances. While in transit, the Uruguayan government learned of the visa scam taking place in Uruguayan consulates throughout Europe and determined they would expel anyone with visas issued on or after December **20th** of that year. Among those Austrian Jews traveling on the ship to Uruguay with the Donners were several families whose visas had been issued after December **20th**. Despite the questionable documents, the Donners were allowed to enter Uruguay.

Herbert, like Eva, arrived in Uruguay not knowing any Spanish. When he left Vienna, he was in the 4th grade, but when he entered Uruguay, he was placed in 1st grade until he could master the language. Herbert's family, like Eva's, settled down in Montevideo to rebuild their lives and eventually gain an economic foothold. As Herbert and Eva learned more about each other's history, interest, and mutual experiences, they agreed to go out with each other after that pivotal first date. They each found it easy to stay talking at one of many cafes along the sidewalks of Avenida 18 de Julio until early mornings, learning about each other's lives and hopes after their losses. They continued to see each other for a few months, cautious about making a commitment. After several months an event took place which brought them closer. The Uruguayan Ambassador to Paraguay, who was well known to Eva's parents met an abrupt death in Asuncion, Paraguay. Eva, well acquainted with the ambassador told Herbert of her plans to attend his viewing. With chivalry and a desire to grow closer to Eva, Herbert proposed to escort Eva to Paraguay. This unanticipated trip which included time with Eva's family and their social circles in Paraguay were among the steps which drew them to a closer bond and friendship.

After their trip to Paraguay the two continued pursuing one another more extensively. Eva viewed this renewed friendship and now a more profound relationship as a welcomed opportunity to move forward with her life. To fill the void left by Bill's death, Eva desired to find some sense of well-being, seeking comfort in recalling meaningful mutual experiences that transpired with Herbert over the intervening years. At the time, neither had it in their minds to engage in a serious relationship. Nonetheless, they felt good together, rejuvenated in their newfound companionship.

A month after the Asuncion trip, Herbert left Montevideo on a trip to Canada and the United States with his daughter, Noemi. At about the same time, Eva also traveled for a month to Pompano Beach, Florida where she had previously planned to stay at the home of some Argentine friends who made their vacation place available to her. While both were in the states, Herbert rang Eva and sought to meet up before her return to Uruguay. Eva agreed and picked him up at the Fort Lauderdale airport. While in Fort Lauderdale, proximate to Eva's place in Pompano Beach they spent several days together growing in their affection and bonds in what Eva described as "a honeymoon." Throughout the few days together, they went on sightseeing trips and dining experiences in this warm touristy area of South Florida. With each outing Eva believed that Herbert had much in common with her. Eva found their chemistry to be desirable and sought out ways to draw Herbert towards her. She felt that each opportunity to share with one another created a means by which to deepen their ties leading towards a more permanent relation.

Upon returning to Montevideo, Eva found that her carefree days with Herbert were gone. News of their relationship spread among their friends and through their social circles, and some of Herbert's relatives opposed what they perceived as a hasty relation and sought to intervene. To avoid controversies, Eva and Herbert continued their meetings in the shadows. Herbert found himself lying to his family, but even though Eva did not feel entirely comfortable either, she hid nothing from her daughters who knew of their close affection and friendship. Eva's mother, however, seemed pleased with Eva's ties with Herbert which brought companionship to her and a welcomed change in her attitude and state of mind. Despite the attraction and companionship, Eva struggled with jealous friends and all forms of gossip. Fearful and conscious of his social status in Montevideo, Herbert retreated and sought to place limits on their encounters. While Eva acquiesced, she also grew bitter, seeing herself as a secreted "lover," rather than friend or fiancée. She found such measures unnecessary as they were both unentangled widows.

Eva's spirits once again declined after experiencing a period of sentimental euphoria and great satisfaction. She could not settle for being Herbert's lover, and she would not hide in the shadows from their children or run to an apartment to shelter from being seen among the neighbors. These thoughts swirled and caused her to derail. Despite Herbert's reassurances that their relationship would overcome the naysayers, Eva doubted if she could thrive in such an unwelcomed environment. Nevertheless, all aspects of their love for one another continued to strengthen as they found comfort in each other's presence. Eva lacked confidence and needed to be prioritized in their relationship.

The summer of 1977 became one of disillusion for Eva. She rented a flat in Punta del Este, but the season did not go as planned. Herbert travelled that summer to Punta as well, but with his kids. Although the kids seldom gave him much attention, they were present, and Herbert would not show himself publicly with Eva. Reluctantly, they resorted to late night meetings in obscure places. This made Eva question her self-worth and brought about feelings of doubt about their relationship. In this time of uncertainty, she questioned her virtue as a parent and success in the male dominated workplace. These feelings deprived her of sleep and brought on lethargy which she could not shake. Herbert seemed to understand her pain and endeavored to reassure her, but he could not fully commiserate with Eva's emotional rollercoaster.

In October of 1977, Eva left for the states with her daughters to attend the wedding of one of Bill's nieces living in Rochester. On their return to Montevideo, Brenda, her eldest, chose to stay back and take up residency in the states. She settled in Florida and determined to marry her fiancée, Roberto. Brenda who bore dual U.S. and Uruguayan citizenship facilitated Roberto's permanent residency once married.

Under her doctor's care and treatment, Eva returned to Montevideo in a much better state of mind. Nonetheless, she lapsed into periods of anxiety when confronting uncertainty. She shared an experience when Herbert's uncle came to Montevideo which reflected her continued insecurities. The uncle visited Herbert annually. On this trip, he met Eva and, in their encounters, made inquiries concerning her prior marriage and social relations. Eva saw this line of questioning as an affront to her fitness to wed Herbert and believed Herbert's former sister-in-law unsuccessfully sought to build a wedge between them by spreading unsubstantiated tales about her. Despite feeling insecure and experiencing continued tension, Eva was not dissuaded from pursuing Herbert.

As their relation continued to flourish, Eva looked for opportunities to draw closer to Herbert's kids, the boys, residing in Montevideo. Herbert's daughter, Noemi, was studying in the states at the time. When Herbert proposed marriage, Eva claims she unraveled and felt the floor move beneath her. She felt apprehensive over his austere nature. Herbert, an engineer was punctilious and disciplined in his affairs. Despite these feelings, she felt completely in love with him. Following his declaration, Herbert began to make plans without consulting Eva, fearing she might back out. He then proposed a trip to Asuncion, Paraguay to celebrate Eva's father's 70th birthday. There, they received Eva's parents' approval who showed pride in introducing them to their social circles as Eva's future husband.

While in Asuncion, Eva found that her mother was not her former self. She looked poorly and acknowledged that she did not feel well. Further, Elsie's relations with Walter remained strident. At this point in her life, Eva knew much about the source of her father and mother's tensions. As most women of that generation, Elsie had learned to cope and accept their marital discourse and "*soldier on*". In the Roth marriage, it had been Elsie who succeeded economically with her relentless work ethic and diligence in establishing the language school.

In January of 1978, Elsie came over from Asuncion to spend her summer in Montevideo, as had been her habit. While in Montevideo, Elsie fell ill and submitted to several medical tests which showed nothing amiss. Later, doctors suggested hepatitis, and, after further testing, decided to hospitalize her to perform an endoscopy. To Eva's great distress, the tests showed Elsie had a malignant tumor lodged in her liver. Eva understood this was an irreversible diagnosis that would result in imminent death. The doctors operated on Elsie for what she was told was an ulcer, but after the operation Elsie, never regained her strength. Elsie convalesced at the Italian Hospital and later in Eva's home for more than two months, but there was no improvement. She continued to decline and lose weight. Amid the emerging calamity, Eva sought to plan her wedding to Herbert and start a new life. She felt torn apart as she watched her mother whom she loved beyond words, her best friend, slip away. Eva felt helpless and unable to share her feelings with her mother. A time of great anguish ensued. Meanwhile, Elsie wanted to return to Asuncion, and she arranged for Elsie's return once she strengthened. Eva shuttled back and forth between Asuncion and Montevideo every two weeks to be with her mom, but each trip became more difficult. Their conversations and talks were filled with unceasing sorrow. Elsie was bright and understood what her body felt, Eva firmly believed her mother knew she was at death's door. She concluded Elsie wanted to spare her from suffering by hiding her pain.

Eva and Herbert set their wedding date for May 25, 1978. They planned a small intimate gathering at Estela's home, Eva's future mother-in-law. There, close friends and family would join them in the celebration. Eva yearned to have her mom present with them. Unable to accept the seriousness of the illness, Eva provided for Elsie to wear a dress at the wedding ordered from Buenos Aires to be delivered to Asuncion. She also arranged for nurses to transport her to the wedding.

Two weeks prior to the wedding Eva traveled to Asuncion to spend a week with her mom and obtain her approval as to the attire which she planned for her to wear at her wedding ceremony. That week, however, Elsie was rushed to the hospital in grave condition. On the morning of Friday, the 12th of May, Eva went over to the hospital to bid her mom farewell before returning to Montevideo. She found it difficult to leave as her mom did not recognize her and appeared odd and swollen. No one warned Eva that Elsie's death was hours away. Eva left Asuncion with the assurance from Elsie's doctors that despite her physical state, she would live for several more weeks, yet. Eva arrived in Montevideo four hours later only to learn that her mom had died at 3 in the afternoon.

Herbert and Debbie accompanied Eva back to Asuncion for the two days that followed, the viewing and funeral. Hundreds came to the house and attended the burial. The days following Eva's return to Uruguay were engulfed with a stream of conflicting emotions while she made final preparations for her wedding. Eva felt torn, profoundly mourning the loss of her mother yet preparing to start a new life with the man she had come to love. These were times when she wished she could speak with her mom and seek her advice, give her a hug, and share her joy. In her grief, she consoled herself with the thought of a visit to Elsie's grave site and further opportunities to honor her life.

Walter remained living in Asuncion after Elsie died, despite Eva's insistence that he move back to Montevideo where he could be cared for by his family and friends. Walter's health had deteriorated, and his life seemed precarious. Although Eva tried to find her father a good retirement home in Asuncion he stubbornly chose to live on his own or perhaps with another in the outskirts of Asuncion. He left no forwarding address, and, for a time, Eva could not locate him. Eva eventually wrote to a post office box some acquaintance provided for her dad and was able to reach him. To her surprise, Walter came to Montevideo in October of 1979, two months before Debbie's wedding. At that time, Walter stubbornly disclosed that he would not attend his granddaughter's wedding. The decision, which lacked a cogent explanation shocked and hurt both Debbie and Eva. Walter was Debbie's last surviving grandparent, and his absence at her wedding left a sour note.

Eva and Herbert left for their honeymoon following their wedding. They travelled to Europe and Israel which Eva described as "A time of fully bonding in complete surrender of one to the other." In Israel, Eva took pleasure meeting Herbert's Israeli family and felt fully accepted as an added member. Curiously, she felt most at home at Herbert's uncle's home more than in any other place throughout her stay; this the same uncle who had made her feel uncomfortable with his prying nature a year before while on his visit to Montevideo. Being in his home and especially with his wife, reminded Eva of the home life of her youth in Austria. It seems she found familiarity with their European ways, German dialect, and old-world customs.

Before returning to Montevideo, the newlyweds stopped in Miami. There they spent time with Brenda who had found her home in the United States. Eva and

Herbert stayed in Miami a few days and attended Brenda and Roberto's Civil wedding ceremony. Although Eva did not feel entirely happy with the union and his ability to support Brenda, she resolved that, going forward, Roberto would be her son-in-law and a part of the family. Over the ensuing months, Eva made an earnest effort to treat Roberto as another of her children. Despite her best efforts, Eva struggled to fulfill her stated goal finding Roberto to be disagreeable toward her as she believed he resented her past opposition to the marriage. Once married, Eva helped them settle in Miami. She continued to provide substantial economic support to both Brenda and Roberto throughout their time together, but their marriage would not last. Roberto wanted to make his mark in the states. He began a career with a major retailer and left for work early only to return late at night. His life became his quest for managerial ascension. Brenda remained, mostly at home and their married life unraveled over time.

Herbert and Eva returned to Montevideo after debating where they would reside and they determined Eva's home in the Pocitos neighborhood would be the best alternative. To make it "their" home, they purchased new furniture for their bedroom and made other cosmetic changes. Debbie remained somewhat awkwardly in the home with them until December 1979 when she married Eduardo in a cheerful and beautiful celebration held at the distinctive Kibon bayside venue near their home in Pocitos.

Eva's first years of marriage to Herbert were blissful, although at times they quarreled about petty matters. There were some minor irritants, such as whether each other's former spouses should have their photos prominently displayed in their home. Eva had some insecurities about Herbert's former spouse and whether he might succumb to a roving eye, but neither of these conjectures were sources of real concern, rather a reflection of Eva's great desire to hold on to Herbert with all her heart. She saw their marriage as a tender and sublime love; all-encompassing, carnally and spiritually. Eva wanted nothing to interfere with this passionate moment in her life. She wanted only to remain faithful to Herbert and for him to do the same.

Shortly after Debbie's wedding, Walter, went into the hospital for a hernia operation. He did not share this with Eva who could have been of support in his recovery. Although the operation was a success, Walter, while trying to rise, unassisted, fell and broke his hip. Upon learning of the fall, Debbie and Eva headed back to Asuncion. The hip injury caused Walter's health to decline rapidly, and he failed to recover. Walter passed away on a Sunday in the early part of March 1980. Similarly, to Elsie's death, Eva did not arrive in Asuncion until after he passed. Walter died alone, abandoned by the woman who had lived in their home and cared for him in the hospital. This woman disappeared with his money and possessions, including his home, a vehicle and the valuables that remained in the Roth home. Elsie had earmarked these as Eva's inheritance, but Eva had never wanted to remove them while Elsie lived.

Eva and Herbert were able to come to Walter's burial which was poorly attended. Eva believed that her father, whom she dearly loved, led a very sad and unfulfilled life. She resented the poor choices he made that led to constant friction and left him isolated as his life came to an end. Eva left Asuncion with a bitter taste in her mouth. The place which she had loved to stay no longer felt warm and welcoming. Eva went back two or three times on short trips, but those cemetery visits were principally to make sure the tomb inscriptions were properly placed and the grave site maintained.

[Scrivener's Note: A few years later, at Eva's request, I visited her parent's gravesites to ensure that they were being properly maintained. The visit was complicated as no one wanted to acknowledge a Jewish Cemetery existed in Asuncion. At the time, strongman, Alfredo Stroessner who ruled Paraguay from 1954 through 1989, had made Paraguay a haven for Nazi war criminals and instituted repressive laws which silenced most of the population. Despite minor inconveniences, the grave markers were located and found to be well maintained.]

The Ground Starts to Quake

"The mystery of human existence lies not in just staying alive, but in finding something to live for." - Fyodor Dostoyevsky, The Brothers Karamazov.

Eva believed some of her disagreements with Herbert were brought about by her malleability. She sought to become as Herbert wanted her to be always doing what pleased him. In time, this began to chafe at her, it seemed a mask. Eva felt that this tension arose from her anxiety and longing for those distant and departed in her family. Her parents were gone, and Debbie and Brenda were living abroad with their husbands. Despite some of these feelings, Eva drew comfort from her strengthening ties with Herbert's children. Eva believed the kids, Hugo, Diego, and Noemi, loved her in their own way. Her greatest battles were in grappling with the youngest, Noemi, who could be short-tempered and rude toward her. As she drew companionship from Herbert and his family, she still pined for her daughters who were far from her. While issues surfaced with both sets of children, Eva and Herbert determined to resolve the problems sharing their concerns and seeking ways to eliminate rifts. No matter their resolution, Eva felt that her daughters were much different from Herbert's children. She could not detach herself from the affection and longing she had for Brenda and Debbie. Debbie and Eduardo had been her source of comfort, particularly when she experienced the loss of her father and mother. Not even Herbert could fill their void.

Herbert shaped their marriage in a manner which differed from Eva's marriage to Bill. Herbert wanted more latitude to engage in sports activities and profession related gatherings. He socialized and cultivated relations with engineers and tradesmen, engaged in his industry. These were activities for which Eva lacked interest. Eva gravitated more towards social interactions which she and Bill had enjoyed together. With Herbert, social gatherings were more formal in nature, and Eva felt threatened by them.

As Eva grew to discover, Herbert's life early on in their marriage included substantial responsibilities over the family business. Upon the Donners' arrival in Montevideo, Herbert's family, which owned a shirt business in Vienna, started up a similar business out of their home. This business succeeded and continued for many years. In 1962, Herbert and his family formed NEOSUL, S.A. This business had a completely different orientation from the former garment factory. NEOSUL focused on the manufacture and sale of vinyl products as well as PCV piping used in irrigation systems. The business became extremely successful but required ongoing managerial attention, international business travel along with time consuming involvement in trade organizations, board appointments, and client development.

For a while, Eva felt isolated from her friends and social groups, and she could not see the logic for her attitude. She gradually worked her way back to her more social, vivacious personality, developing her own interest in philanthropy and rekindling her friendships and travels. She also continued her work at Swan, Culbertson, and Fritz well into the 1980s. Despite having jointly set up their own places in Montevideo and Punta as their own "love nest," she felt restless. In time, Eva and Herbert made space for one another and settled into a comfortable rhythm which accommodated their blended families.

Herbert's children each took very different paths. By the early 1980s, Hugo, the eldest, was well entrenched in NEOSUL and his engineering background assured him a long-term future with the business which continued to grow over the years. Hugo remained with NEOSUL until his retirement from active participation around 2020. As of 2023, NEOSUL averaged annual sales of US$1.3 million per Dunn & Bradstreet. The middle child, Diego, born the same year as Debbie, became a renown contemporary abstract painter. His exploration of art mediums led him on a journey into ancient eastern religions and meditative mystical practices, and his art gained international recognition. Noemi the youngest, married Marcel Branaa, a Uruguayan tanning and leather industrialist.

Eva's daughters, Brenda and Deborah, both married, moved to the United States, and made their own way. Both were fluent in English when they moved to the states, but their respective husbands, Roberto and Eduardo were not. Both husbands embraced the United States with drive and enthusiasm and quickly gained employment to provide for their spouses. Brenda's marriage to Roberto would be short lived while Deborah's remains lasting and enduring. As Eva's daughters' lives became entrenched in the United States, Eva found great pleasure in frequent trips to the United States.

Eva's passion for travel never wavered. Soon after her marriage to Herbert, she traveled on an excursion through the Nile and the Aswan Dam. Her daughters followed this trip closer than any other as grave political events in the Middle East coincided with her travels.Eva traveled in September 1981 through Israel then Egypt as the High Holidays approached. As her excursion boat approached Cairo, on October 6th, news hit the wires that Anwar Sadat, Prime Minister of Egypt had been assassinated, the day before Yom Kippur. Deborah and Brenda's hearts sank when they heard the news. They feared that tensions would erupt in the region and Eva would be in peril. Egypt sought to control the narrative concerning the death of its leader and immediately instituted a complete news black-out. Phones, cables, and other forms of communication were shut down leaving the family to pray and wait for news to percolate. A couple of days later, Eva spoke with her daughters by telephone and reassured them of her safety before returning to Montevideo days later.

As the children settled into their lives, Eva and Herbert took time to enjoy their life of travel abroad on a frequent basis. There were trips to Israel that often coincided with the high holidays, vacations to Santorini, London, France and Australia where Eva still had relatives and other pleasurable islands in various parts of the globe.

In 1985, Debbie and Eduardo shared the good news that a child was on the way. This would be Eva's first grandchild and Eva, as well as Herbert, were elated. Daniel was born in 1985 and the Donners came state-side to help select the Mohel and partake in the bris. After the birth, Debbie reached out to her trusted childhood nanny, Maria, who travelled from Uruguay to help care for her beautiful boy. Eva felt comforted that Maria would be a loving caretaker to this child after Debbie returned to work at the conclusion of her maternity leave.

After Danny's birth, Eva's travels to the United States became a premier destination. As a result, Eva purchased a condominium in a high rise in Turnberry, a glitzy community in North Dade County, Florida facing the intercostal waterway. The condominium provided a life of sun and fun and social outings and events within their new community. The condo made for a pleasurable haven and allowed them to visit Debbie and Brenda while on holidays. With their presence well established, the Donners could enjoy year-round fun in the sun. This benefitted Eva who would continue to vacation in Punta del Este and then travel to Florida's temperate climate during the Uruguayan winters.

Debbie and Ed's marriage flourished with two additional loves: Jacqueline born in 1989 and Alejandro four years later. All three of Eva's grandchildren obtained college degrees and have flourished in their chosen careers. Danny obtained a master's degree in business administration and chose to follow his mother's path into banking and finance He also married a jovial, artsy and well-educated Ecuadorian woman and had a young child and another in on the way. Both excel in their respective professions. Jacqueline studied fashion in the prestigious Fashion Institute of Technology New York and married Nick Haller, a graduate of Manhattan college and a true New Yorker with an avocation for impressive cuisine. The two are making a life in New York in their chosen professions in fashion merchandizing and global commercial insurance. Both welcomed their first child, a daughter in 2025. The youngest, Alejandro, has become a respected and well-known personality in the Florida sports broadcast markets. He is engaged to be married to Valentina, a compassionate nurse and enterprising esthetician.

Brenda did not have any children. In 1980, Brenda and Debbie lived in the same development with their respective husbands. Brenda lived with Roberto until their marriage soured and they chose to divorce. After her divorce Brenda looked to make her own way. For a short while she found joy in dog-walking and caring for dogs, but she would need to find a way to support herself going forward. With Eva's support and encouragement, she enrolled in a course to become a make-up artist. She dreamed of making it as a celebrity makeup artist. Regrettably, Brenda lacked the connections to enter this competitive, and at times cut-throat field and settled for working as a make-up artist for a major cosmetic brand.

While continuing to search for direction, Brenda bounced through bad relationships which offered her no security or future. Seeing no daylight in Miami, Brenda boldly decided to load up her most valuable possessions into the back of her car and drive cross-country on her own to California. She settled in Sunnyvale, about an hour south of San Francisco. There she continued working in the cosmetics industry while searching for a sense of purpose and stability. After bumpy relations, she met a man who would bring back her joy, Guillermo Toro-Lira Stahl. Guillermo, a Peruvian industrial designer and writer who lived in the states for many years, was also divorced and had adult children. Guillermo has a passion for history, particularly that pertaining to the origins of Pisco from pre-colonial days in Spain through South America and onward to San Francisco. Over the years, he has written and published several books and articles on this subject. Guillermo fell in love with Brenda and asked her to marry him. He has become her anchor and given happiness and purpose to her life. They remained living in Sunnyvale for several years, while often traveling to Peru and the far east and Europe. Abroad, Guillermo and Brenda shared and expanded his vast knowledge of the history of Pisco and Pisco Sour and its seeds in San Francisco. They now split residences between Florida and Peru.

Eva continued to love and support her two daughters through the ensuing years. Eva and Herbert's relations, however, became strained with each year. In 1996, both came up from Uruguay to joyfully celebrate their grandson Danny's Bar Mitzvah at a trendy venue in Miami called Signature Gardens. The Bar Mitzvah, well attended by Donner faithful and relatives from out of state, boasted musicians and entertainers (ringers). Daniel played the drums to this extravagant gathering overflowing with food and drinks for all to enjoy. The older guests were most generous, and Danny experienced one of his most memorable life events. Six years later Jacqueline celebrated her Bat Mitzvah at the same venue with the theme of "Mall Madness." Her party also had many guests including the cousins from New York and their Rochester family, but the older Donner guests were absent, including Herbert. Jacqueline's party provided a glimpse into her future interests and goals. As Jacqueline grew, she remained passionate about fashion, an interest she attributes wholly to Eva. Upon graduating from high school, she chose to study in New York and determined to break with the south and make a home in New York City. Alex's Bar Mitzvah would come four years later. His party had a more informal atmosphere with many of his and his parent's friends in attendance. By Alex's Bar Mitzvah Eva's life had changed, and Herbert no longer played a part in it.

The years after separating from Herbert were devastating for Eva and she sought solace in travels and visits with old friends. Hoping to shed her lonely state, she came to New York and New Jersey where she laid bare her desperate need for companionship and affection. On that trip, she found no joy or pleasure in any one thing or place, but, like a tumbleweed, kept moving without direction or purpose. As part of that trip, she walked through Atlantic City and entered the casinos which provide neither the light of day nor the darkness of night. Here, she filled her head with the noise of clanging bells emitted by slot machines and the dealers luring the somnambulant into yet another game of chance. This place seemed reflective of Eva's mood -melancholic and empty. As she walked in and out of several casinos, she peered at the kitschy stores along the boardwalk but found no pleasure and, after a while, grew tired and bored. Eva's brief visit to New Jersey provided a little companionship but also reflected her need for something to fill her life. In her state of mind, she would seek to satisfy her void with some urgency.

Eva sought to again find happiness in other relationships. Lurking in the background were unscrupulous individuals who sought to take advantage of her vulnerabilities and her kind and generous heart. While she may have understood that she was being exploited, she also felt a desperate need to be embraced and loved as she had once been. Cristina, Eduardo's sister and confidant, tipped-off Debbie and Eduardo as to her observations and commentaries in and around Montevideo concerning those preying on Eva. Debbie and Brenda both saw the abuse and dangers and tried to protect their mother as much as possible from herself. Debbie, now well entrenched as a banking professional, sought to shelter Eva's assets and set safeguards in place. Both daughters met resistance from a combative Eva who still saw herself as a sharp businesswoman in control of her life and circumstances.

In 2015, Debbie, seeing her mother's emotional state and decline, urged Eva to move to the United States and live in a place of her choosing. Eva still clung to the delusion that her last and most damaging love cared for her. In a few years, this last relation gained a foothold into Eva's assets and finances and inflicted irreversible losses. When little was left to plunder, he fled.

Eva's last years were spent living with Debbie and Eduardo with the aid of a caretaker. Over those years, Eva showed progressive signs of dementia and the onset of Alzheimer's Disease. Debbie endeavored to find the most respected medical experts and treatments which could arrest the continuing decline in Eva's mental and emotional state, but nothing could be done. These were difficult years for Debbie and Brenda who collaborated on ways to provide for their mother. Eduardo, for his part, shuttled back and forth to Uruguay to secure Eva's property and administer the disposition of her remaining assets.

As Eva grew feeble, and at times argumentative, Debbie sought ways to provide for her mother while continuing to work and maintain her home life. She researched several assisted living facilities all with some limitations. Then G-d provided a place less than two blocks from Debbie's home that afforded compassionate care. This care facility brought the family opportunities to visit Eva frequently and share life events and holidays with her as she continued to deteriorate.

Deborah and Eduardo Solana Wedding

Eva, Brenda, and Guillermo Toro-Lira

Eduardo, Mary Gross, Eva, and Deborah in Rochester, New York

Eva with Alex, Danny, and Jackie in Miami, Florida

Alex, Danny, Jackie, Deborah, Lucila, Cristina, and William in Montevideo, Uruguay

Deborah with Eva Roth

WE ARE ALL ON A JOURNEY

In September of 2022, Eva and her family celebrated the High Holy Days and commemorated the Jewish New Year 5783. Brenda came up to Miami with Guillermo, and Jackie sought to take a short break from work to come down to Miami and visit her grandmother. The family all took turns spending time with Eva at the assisted living facility for the last few months of her life.

Debbie had let all those close to her believe Eva was on the decline. However, the days just prior to Rosh Hashanah, Eva seemed more animated than in the past. Having just returned from High Holiday services at the Temple, the family appeared to be in high spirits. Eva seemed alert, but not too interested in food, not even sweets. Some tried to coax her with a cookie but with no success. Then she began to speak mostly unconnected words which did not amount to a conversation, but as she heard her daughters' voices, she was moved to hum a song and smiled broadly when efforts were made to sing a verse of "Avenu, Malkainu." That afternoon, the family left encouraged. Jackie received reassurances that her grandmother's condition did not appear grave in nature. The reassurance would be misplaced, but Jackie considered the matter and determined to come down to Florida later in the month. That evening, the family partook in a festive dinner and celebrated the blessed day.

A few days later, Eva's spirit rebounded. The assisted living facility manager put out a brief video showing Eva's willingness to eat on her own and showing signs of strengthening. This would be a short-lived recovery, and, on the morning of October 12, Abba took Eva to her final resting place.

In Judaism, the sages counsel that one must not overly praise the departed in eulogy. This is because tradition says angels will meet before G-d and report on what is said of the departed. Mourners are to simply share a modest remembrance of a loved one since the day will come when G-d "will swallow up death forever, and the Lord G-d will wipe away tears from all faces..." Isaiah 25:8. This is the great hope of Jewish believers. Forgoing the eulogy, Jews are left to recount stories and memories of those whom they have loved and recalled.

Four weeks after Eva left this life, her body was transported to Uruguay where she wanted to be buried with her beloved Bill, father to her daughters, at the British Cemetery in Montevideo.

Most of the immediate family travelled down to Uruguay for the burial. Ed and his sister, Cristina made accommodation arrangements for the family. Several stayed in a centrally located hotel while Danny and his family stayed with Cristina's daughter Luchi. Debbie and Brenda arranged for a Shabbat service at the synagogue Eva once attended, to be held the day prior to the burial. They also worked with the British Cemetery staff to arrange for the opening of Bill's crypt and Eva's burial. Several of Eva's lifelong friends attended the Shabbat service which allowed Debbie and Brenda to grieve, reminisce among friends and family. The perceptive rabbi crafted and delivered a sensitive message to those in attendance. He understood those present at Eva's synagogue included Jews as well as Gentiles. During his message, he accomplished the dual goals of comforting and reassuring the family while carefully sharing the customs and rituals accompanying a Jewish death and burial.

That evening and the following morning, the family tried to put together a message for the gravesite which would honor Eva's life. In the end, Alex, the youngest grandson, was unable to travel to Uruguay but sent his message which captured the family's pain and sorrow but also pride and joy in recalling her love, generosity, and impact on the life of her family and friends.

Alex's tribute to his grandmother delivered remotely:

Today my grandmother Eva is being laid to rest in Uruguay. A difficult time for the Solanas, Melvins, and Toro-Liras who are all together in Montevideo celebrating her life. Unfortunately, I am unable to attend, so I wanted to share some thoughts on her life, legacy, and impact.

Eva was born in Vienna, Austria, in 1933. A few years later, her entire family was forced to escape Austria due to the rise of Nazism. My grandmother was only six years old when her father, mother, and grandparents attempted their escape. Their first attempt failed. A second attempt at escaping was successful, though challenging. Traveling west through Europe with no real plan, just hope, and a belief in humanity to help find safety in an environment that was anything but safe for a group of Jews who left everything behind other than what they could carry on their person.

A dangerous, yet successful mission, with the help of others, led the Roth's across Europe and on to a shipping liner headed for South America where yet another challenge awaited.

Eva's family were not certain they'd be welcomed in a part of the world they'd never visited, but the risk of staying in a war-torn Europe was greater than jumping on a tiny ocean liner across the Atlantic searching for uncertain refuge. Their first attempt at disembarking in Brazil was unsuccessful. Denied entry because of their status as Jews (lacking adequate visas and entry permits). Their last hope was a small country they had probably never heard of Uruguay.

When their ship arrived in the Port of Montevideo, once again, the lack of valid Visas stood in their way. A family with no money was left to await their return to Europe where they'd surely be intercepted and brought back to eventual incarceration and probably death. In a turn of events, a small Jewish community in Montevideo got word of the Jewish family who was hoping for a last chance at freedom. Hours before the ship was scheduled for its return trip, a deal was made to sneak her family off the ship.

This small community had nothing to gain by helping my grandmother's family, but their selfless efforts proved to be monumental. Not only were they now granted a safe exit from the ship, this six-year-old and her family were given the resources to find shelter, learn a new language, and begin working in a foreign land.

I often reflect on this voyage my grandmother's family undertook and the hardships they faced just to be able to live. How many people I'll never be able to thank that risked their lives to help an Austrian family find safety. A small community in this tiny South American country, for no other reason than to do the right thing, that helped pave the way for my grandmother to live an incredible life and build a family in different parts of the world.

We turn on the news, scroll through our feeds, discuss amongst each other how awful this world can be at times, but I hold on to this memory as a reflection of how good people can be and what it can lead to.

My love for Eva, and her family whom I never met, undertaking a near-impossible task can't be understated. To that tiny Jewish community in a country, I now call my second home – Uruguay - words can't describe the gratitude and indebtedness I feel. That identity of being a Uruguayan-Jew is one I will always carry with me.

Proudly, Danny read this heartfelt, all-encompassing message at the grave site while Alex participated from the states. Danny, together with most in attendance, choked back tears and hugged one another. They then left the cemetery to spend a couple of hours eating and recalling the life of this incredible woman. These parting gatherings brought closure to the family and allowed each to grieve in their own way in the days that followed. The lasts days as a family in Uruguay were spent in Eva's flat in Punta del Este before each returned to their respective homes.

In 2024, Debbie, Ed, Brenda, Guillermo and some of the grandchildren returned to Uruguay to commemorate Eva's first Yahrzeit. For Debbie and Brenda, Eva remains the mom who loved and cared for them. Eva provided for their education and transition to the United States. Debbie's business savvy, acumen, and leadership in her profession is forged by the example her mother provided. Brenda inherited her mom's passion for fashion, jewelry, and the arts. These legacies became the fabric of the things that appealed and brought joy to Eva while she lived. Through Eva and their grandparents, Debbie and Brenda embraced a love for Judaism and its rich heritage of traditions and celebrations which has been passed to her grandchildren. They embrace a zeal for the state of Israel and its right to exist proudly proclaiming, "*Am Yisrael Chai*". Each year they share and celebrate in the most significant holidays, if not in shul, then at home. While both are married to non-Jews, their spouses, like Bill, have embraced the culture and their love for Judaism. Debbie has passed these traditions on to her children which now springs up in her grandson and perhaps those yet to come.

Eva left those who loved her a world of joyful memories. Although she experienced a life of searing events, great suffering, and fear, her family's experience, together with her own, reflect an indominable spirit to not just survive, but to live and share in all the bounties our Creator has provided. Eva worked hard in her life and acquired wisdom and understanding from those she loved and those she encountered in her Jewish community along the way. She used these attributes to persevere and grow, even during periods of anxiety and adversity. Her daughters, grandchildren, and great-grandson always remained her crowning glory. She leaves a legacy of philanthropy, generosity of heart, business acumen, and *joie de vivre*. Throughout her adult life, she travelled and discovered the world. She danced, sang, and shared the joy, pathos, and intense appreciation of the theater, arts, and music of all dimensions. She sprinkled her wealth, insights, and generosity with her family and her friends. Those who had the privilege of being touched by Eva are all the wiser and better for it.

For those who remain, it is a legacy to impart to the next generation.

ACKNOWLEDGEMENTS

This chronicle of the life of a dear sweet friend and mentor is the product of interviews with Eva while her mind was crisp and filled with the details of her long and blessed life. These were supplemented by her writings from 1984 that sought to record her life's journey and family life in Uruguay. I thank those who provided background and research, including Ruth Kon, Eva's dear friend, who survives her and remains clear about milestones of their friendships, Julie Drexel who provided detailed background information pertaining to Eva's family and ancestry, Mary Gross who shared family history pertaining to Bill Melvin and his family, and, most importantly, I thank Debbie, Eva's daughter, who cautiously guarded and preserved all the letters, recordings, documents, and photographs her mother assembled and kept throughout her life.

Additional details were preserved in a video recorded as part of Danny's Bar Mitzvah project in which he interviewed his grandparents, Eva and Herbert.

I also thank Brenda Melvin who recalled much about their visits to Paraguay and time spent with Eva's parents, Walter and Elsie.

I undertook research from materials available through the United States Holocaust Memorial Museum in Washington D.C. and *Yad Vashen*, The World Holocaust Remembrance Center in Jerusalem, Israel.

POSTSCRIPT

In the late 70s, Eva Roth invited Debbie, Eduardo, and me to Uruguay. Her welcoming smile took us through the Carrasco Montevideo Airport terminal as if it were her own parlor. The whole country was her home. She drove a small but trendy European Opel, driving as if she could command the streets of Montevideo. This trip introduced the world of Eva Roth Donner, a successful businesswoman, philanthropist, zealous advocate for the state of Israel and a Uruguayan socialite.

At the time, Eva worked at an office in the Greco-Uruguaya building located at 1481 Misiones Street, in the old city part of Montevideo, just a few blocks from the port. She worked as an investment manager and private banker alongside her assistant, Leonor.

Carrasco airport looked to me like the small city airport in the United States. Passengers walked down a movable staircase mounted onto the airplane's door and were greeted by smartly dressed personnel ushering them from the tarmac onto the terminal. On a crisp cold Uruguayan winter day, Debbie's mom met her at the airport, warmly dressed and beaming with excitement at the sight of her daughter and son-in-law. Eva provided a welcoming city tour into the city market, known as El Mercado del Puerto. This former port terminal building provided a gastronomic and cultural experience. In this rustic cavernous building, her guests experienced an extraordinary display of meats of various cuts and savory sausages. The aromatic odors of charcoal and tanned leather soaked the air. Eva carefully planned the outings, showing only the best of its culture and history. She reluctantly drove through the shantytown part of El Cerro. Afterwards, she confidently proclaimed that this section of town did not represent the lifestyle in her country. This for me was the introduction to the "Switzerland of South America!" I had read about in library books.

Eva drove through the upper-crust neighborhoods of the suburb of Carrasco before entering Montevideo proper. She toured city beaches along the route entering the suburb of Pócitos. This urban center filled with a mixture of homes and small to midsize apartment buildings appeared an odd place for a beach. I struggled to comprehend that the beautiful sandy beaches were the shores of the Rio de la Plata, not some part of the Atlantic.

The Donner home sat on the corner of Teru, just a couple of blocks from Mahatma Gandhi Boulevard, known as the "rambla". Artwork covered most of the mahogany paneled walls of the living room. Likewise, paintings and sculptures dressed up each room. The wood burning fragrance emitted from a fireplace permeated the air of the home providing a comforting warmth.

On this trip, Debbie happily shared warm memories of long summers in Punta del Este, the vast beach resort in the eastern point of Uruguay. This beach resort city-center boasted fashionable stores and trendy coffee shops with few patrons. The drive in through the resort town reflected a tapestry of manicured gardens with most of the town's folk moving about appearing to be servants, maintenance workers, and anglers. Many of the residences and businesses were shuttered for the winter. During the days in Punta, Debbie and her family enjoyed brisk, blustery walks on the beach and its boardwalks.

This trip concluded with an unforgettable weekend in Buenos Aires which Eva and her husband Herbert arranged. There, a short cab ride took us to our boutique hotel aptly named, "Hotel Buenos Aires," just a few meters from Argentina's seat of power, the Casa Rosada. The cab ride through a wide boulevard lined with fountains and parks ushered us into a Paris-like city filled with outdoor cafes, beautiful gardens, and statues of fallen heroes. Our small hotel rooms had a bird's eye view into the Plaza de Mayo which led into the Casa Rosada and Parque Colon.

During that weekend, the family took a touristy boat ride on the Rio de la Plata. That night, Eva showed off her and Herbert's skills on the dance floor. Their sensual looks and subtle gliding gestures portrayed the beauty of the milonga, a slower version of the tango.

Prior to leaving Buenos Aires, Eva invited everyone to a classical music concert at the Teatro Colon, one of the world's most renowned opera houses. This experience seemed a dreamy conclusion to the trip. Our seats were boxed seats several flights above the orchestra pit. The next day we returned to Montevideo.

This trip to Uruguay provided a window into a generous, kind woman, European in tastes and style but well entrenched in her South American lifestyle. She shared a broad knowledge of regional politics and economies. Her successes the outgrowth of opportunities in a broadminded country that had welcomed the Roth family to live freely, work and study. The doors opened to them allowed

Eva to grow with tenacity and determination. With confidence she went on to become an enterprising businesswoman. Her business acumen allowed her to succeed and provide for many in need. Her generosity will endure in those she loved and the charities and causes she supported.

About the Author

Isabel C Balboa, received her BA and MBA from Barry University and JD from Rutgers, the State University of New Jersey. This book is the compilation of many hours of interviews with Eva Roth Donner, her daughters, and grandchildren over the course of 15 years. The interviews were supplemented by a number of documents, notebooks and letters that Eva preserved throughout her life.

www.ingramcontent.com/pod-product-compliance
Lightning Source LLC
LaVergne TN
LVHW020045110826
845155LV00029B/636

* 9 7 8 1 9 4 5 4 9 3 7 3 7 *